NATURE
&
NURTURE

A Journey Through
the Fog of Parenting

For making me
learn how to spell
boutonniere...

Matt Brand

BRAND
NAME
PRESS

ISBN: 978-1-60427-206-2
e-ISBN: 978-1-60427-860-6

Printed and bound in the U.S.A. Printed on acid-free paper.
10 9 8 7 6 5 4 3 2 1

"Without family, you've got nothing."
—Dom Toretto from *The Fast and the Furious*

To Julianna, Chloe, Bev, Lenny, Corey, Dave, Barry,
David, Larissa, Beth, and my entire family:
Thank you for paving the road I travel every day.

To Deanne:
I know you wanted me to eventually write this. Hopefully,
there's a bookstore nearby with this in stock.

To Danyael:
I'm not a dad without you. I'm not the husband and
partner I am without you. Always my queen.

Table of Contents

Foreword

I've known my dad for my whole life—literally. Having a father like him was such a fun experience growing up. I've inherited some amazing qualities from my father, such as my hilarious sense of humor and my incredible athletic ability. For as long as I can remember, my father has written blog posts about my sister and me. When I found out he was going to use all these stories and turn them into a book, I was so excited. This has been my dad's dream for so long and I could not be prouder! I'm so happy that your love of reading while you were growing up inspired you to write a book, Dad!

Love you and congratulations.

Julianna (16 years old)

Today is March 1, 2024. To set the scene, it's currently a quarter to nine as I start this writing. At approximately 7:30 p.m., my dad told my sister and me about his plan to try to publish this book. Both my sister and I had no clue that our dad—who we're both extremely close with—had ever dreamed of publishing a book. He told us that this had been a dream of his for about 10 years. As unexpected as this was, I immediately jumped at the opportunity to write one of the forewords, since writing has always been a strong passion of mine. Speaking of which, I thought I would tell you a bit about my past with writing, how that is even relevant now, and how my writing has influenced my future in many positive ways.

The first book I attempted to write was supposed to be called "New Girl." When I began writing it, I was 8 years old and in the second grade. I have always enjoyed writing, even when it was my friends' least favorite subject. Although I only made it through 13 pages, I think that was pretty impressive for a girl who was that young and had only gone through three years of writing and reading classes. The first few chapters I wrote went a bit like this: A girl moved to a new school, met new friends, rode horses, had two dogs, solved mystery cases, was close with her parents, and so on. I believe that the short story that I began writing foreshadowed my life in a major way. In the past six years since I stopped writing it, every few months or so I go back and read it over and say to myself, "This is kind of like the life I'm living now." Not only did I merely get through 13 pages—my lucky number—but I truly became a new girl. In the past few years, many major things in my life have changed that all go back to these chapters I once wrote. Old friends that grew apart made way for new friends that grew even closer, riding horses gave way to playing field hockey and tennis, having just one dog turned into having two dogs, reading class led to language and literature class and then honors English, but most importantly, my bonds with my family have grown stronger than they've ever been and my dad has upgraded from writing short little blog entries to writing a 250-page book summarizing his experience so far as my (and my sister's) dad.

The writing that I did when I was younger reminds me a lot of the writing that my father has been doing recently. All I can remember from when I was younger about his blog posts was that every year on my birthday, he would show me the post he had written for me. He would talk about my accomplishments during the year leading up to that day as well as how much I'd grown. Growing up to me means maturing, and maturing to me means realizing that a part of me will always be a part of my dad, and looking up to him will always be a daily occurrence that will always end up leading me in the right direction, except of course when he insists on karate fighting or blatantly farts without explanation. This book is a huge accomplishment and I will forever be proud of wherever this goes, no matter what.

Sincerely,

Chloe (14 years old)

Prologue

Being a father is not how I imagined it.

When my wife, Danyael, was pregnant with our first daughter, I—being the type of person who definitely likes to learn as much about as many things as possible and who does not like surprises—did a lot of reading and research about babies and parenthood in general.

I searched for books or articles about anything related to being a parent, from learning about what a woman goes through during pregnancy, to how the fetus develops from week to week, to understanding what types of foods are good to eat and what kinds of behaviors I should expect to witness, as well as information about baby strollers currently in trend, popular names from the past decade, how hospitals work, and what to expect during my wife's labor. If there was something to learn about anything related to this adventure, I was interested.

The problem I encountered was that I had a very difficult time finding anything written from or for the perspective of a dad. So, while I could read a book about *how you'll be feeling in the first trimester* or an article about *what cream to use to help prevent stretch marks*, there wasn't much about *you're going to be a dad, here's what you need to know.* In many cases, what I read was actually quite disconcerting. Many articles had a tone that felt a bit *anti-me.* For instance, there was one article I read that I thought was about baby tantrums but was actually about how the author wanted to blame her husband for everything.

It had lines like, "I was in a store shopping with my baby, and she was having a full meltdown. I couldn't figure out what was wrong. After confirming that she had a clean and dry diaper, wasn't hungry, and didn't need to burp, I called my husband, only to find out that he had introduced a new food without telling me. It was all his fault."

I'm exaggerating a bit, but most of what I read made me feel that way (perhaps I was being too sensitive), and I frankly don't blame them. People write from their own perspective, and I think it's simply that there were very few—if any—blogs or books by dads that are about dads and for dads. Please don't jump down my throat. There is plenty of airspace and there are plenty of words for everyone. I was just trying to be as prepared as possible so I could do the best job as a husband and parent.

Ultimately, this was the reason why I decided to start writing a parenting blog of my own. I wrote my first post for that blog in 2010. I had a few goals when I started it:

- I wanted a journal for myself so I could look back someday and remember all the big moments.
- I thought that maybe, just maybe, if there are other dads out there who went through a similar *research plan* only to find that they couldn't find anything relatable, well, maybe this could be that. I even thought that if other dads wanted to write their own posts, that would be even better.
- Maybe someday, I thought, I could build some sort of parent community where people wrote about their own adventures.

I made a few rules for myself:

1. The first rule was that *I would use my own voice*. For people who know me, I suspect you can hear me in the words. For people who don't, maybe it's a little informal or unusual to read things that are designed to be more *conversational*. I hope you enjoy what you're about to read in the coming chapters.

2. The second rule was to *be authentic*. I wanted to be present in all the moments of parenthood and then reflect on what that was like for me. I didn't ever want to fabricate stories, therefore, everything I would write, glamorous or otherwise, would be what actually happened (well, mostly—see the fourth rule).

3. The third rule was that *I wouldn't create any sort of schedule for writing*. A lot of people who write for a living make it a point, like working out, to have a rigid schedule. I think that would be great for me too, and while I love a good schedule, this rule contributes to the reason that the second rule works. I would write when an idea struck me. Basically, if I had an emotional response or felt strongly about some event that I just witnessed or experienced as a parent, that would be the reason to write. There were some years when I wrote three posts the whole year and other years when I wrote 10.

4. The fourth rule was *to protect my children*. This is a broader rule. I always tried to be careful to write about things that would not violate their privacy. I didn't want to write about anything that they might look back on someday and feel truly embarrassed. I certainly wouldn't want them to be angry with me for sharing something that they thought violated their trust. Certainly, they wouldn't mind if, in 2040, they look back and read an old post about how they liked to read or how potty training went for them.

5. This last rule is ultimately what brought me to this book—
    never write about their thoughts on relationships and part-
    ners, nor about their thoughts on alcohol or drugs. I have
    been writing about my daughters on the blog for 13 years.
    As they've gotten older (15 and 16 at the time I'm writ-
    ing this), the things I could share that are the parallels
    to when they were, say, 4 and 5 years old, are almost
    all things that would violate the fourth rule. I've never
    felt comfortable writing about whatever their thoughts
    are on relationships and partners, so I wouldn't do that.
    What about when they get to the stage where they might
    dabble in drinking alcohol or trying marijuana in any
    of its forms? I wouldn't write about that either. While
    I could ask their permission each time, it started to feel
    tedious and less authentic or organic.

I recently had a realization that the blog, in the form that it took
over the previous 13 years, had to end. There's just not a lot that
I could write about them anymore that would feel *safe.* Once
I had that realization, I thought about how to wrap it up. I've
always wanted to write a book and have been throwing ideas
around for the past 10 years. How do I end the blog? I should
write a book that is a highlight reel of my experience as a parent
so far. I should write a book that not only has revised content
from the blog over the years, but also new thoughts and feelings
on all of those topics.

So that's what I did. I thought about different kinds of ideas
for how to string this all together in a way that maintains the
mission and the rules. I wanted to put together something that
would be fun to read, while also being thoughtful, sad in spots,
and even a little ridiculous from time to time.

Oh, one more rule I forgot: I told myself I wanted to be very
mindful *to not be prescriptive.* I am not a doctor or a child psy-
chologist. I'm just a person who, when I started, was a new parent

trying to figure it out like so many other people. I set out to consciously write about my own experiences, and if people found that relatable or funny or useful, that's great. And, what if they didn't? There are plenty of other places on the internet to spend their time.

My story is not wild and crazy. "Nature & Nurture: A Journey Through the Fog of Parenting" is a collection of my thoughts and experiences from being a parent. There are stories that range from the time my daughters were born all the way through to where they are now—in high school. There are even a few original poems I've written and some stories about me because I figured a little background about who I am might add some context.

I am by no means an expert on parenting. If you are a parent, I'm sure you have your own experiences as well. It is worth noting that my wife and I have always worked together in our effort to make sure we were giving consistent messages to our daughters. While we have not always agreed on how to approach this specific issue or that particular conversation, we always support each other. You might agree with some of the ways we've approached our parenting adventures and you might disagree. I'm *okay* with that. I'm not preaching that you should or shouldn't do anything the way we've done it or the way we'll continue to do it. My goal isn't to *convert* you to or to espouse my philosophy on parenting. It's simply my set of experiences and my opinions, and maybe some of it will be relatable. Maybe some of it will make you laugh. Maybe some of it will make you cry. Maybe some of it will make you think I'm an idiot. I'm *okay* with all of that.

As a child, I was into a lot of what would be considered nerdy things. I loved computers, gadgets, Transformers, and Star Wars. I've also always been fascinated by how things worked. My mother would tell you a story about how when I was a toddler, someone gave me a kid-sized tool belt with a few tools, including a screwdriver. One day I decided that I wanted to take the railings off the steps in our split-level house just because it seemed like a fun thing to do (don't worry: I put them back on the steps). Figuring things out has always been fun and challenging for me. Parenting is no different. I am a confident person, but not so confident as to believe that I know all the answers in any one area.

I am always trying to learn and always trying to improve as a husband and as a parent. As nerdy as I am, I've also regularly had urges to express myself creatively. While writing software professionally allows for a certain type of creativity, writing in this way has also been fun for me and has scratched a different kind of itch.

Where the nerd who is actually more of an introvert takes over is when I start to feel anxious about the idea of putting something I worked on out into the world for people whom I don't know and wondering why anyone would care or if anyone would even read it. I learned fairly early on in the blog's life that it didn't really matter to me who was looking at it; that it was simply an exercise that made me feel good, therefore, it was worth doing. If other people got anything out of it, that was a bonus. As a matter of fact, if you remember the original intent of the blog (to perhaps have a place for dads like me to write about their experiences and in some way to give a perspective that might be useful for other dads), it turned out that my audience was mostly made up of people who weren't dads. Many of the people I've heard from over the years who have found useful or enjoyed what I've written on the blog have been moms or even people who don't have any kids yet but hope to at some point.

Whomever you are, you're welcome here. Whatever your opinions and perspectives are on parenting, you're welcome here. Thank you for getting this far (full-disclosure: you're not that far yet).

I hope you enjoy "Nature & Nurture."

—Matt

PS No, I will not have the sex talk with your kids.

PPS I asked Julianna and Chloe for title suggestions. Julianna told me that sometimes, when she needs to write essays for school, she'll put a filler title in like, "[INSERT TITLE HERE]." Sometimes, she told me, she even forgot to replace it. She then told me that I should just call it "[parenty title here]," but I had to make sure I used the brackets. That was the working title for quite a while because I thought it was cute. I spent quite a bit of time trying to think of a title that was more representative of how this book tells the story about my parenting experience.

About Matt

Matt Brand is a husband and a father of two teenage daughters. He is a self-proclaimed (and others-proclaimed) nerd, a professional software engineer, an elected member of his local school board, and a life-long summer camp person. He believes he is a funny person, but his daughters think he is "mostly cringe." Matt and his daughters agree to disagree. He has been writing about his parenting experience for 15 years, but *Nature & Nurture: A Journey Through the Fog of Parenting* is his first book. He and his family live in the Boston area.

PART I

Beginning

CHAPTER ONE

Birth 1.0—Age 0

March 22, 2008, approximately 1:30 p.m.

"Either I just pissed in my pants or my water just broke." That's what Danyael said to me standing in the produce section of the grocery store. The next few minutes played out like it does in the movies. I got all frantic and said something like, "Are you serious?" She was just about a week beyond the due date so we knew it could happen at any time.

It was a nice Saturday afternoon and we had nothing better to do aside from wait for the arrival so we went out to lunch at a barbecue restaurant near where we live and then decided to go grocery shopping. Danyael had gone to the bathroom (which happened quite frequently during that time) while I started squeezing melons in the produce section.

"Well, I don't know what's happening but I just peed and as soon as I pulled my pants up I either peed again or my water broke."

"Does it hurt? Are you in any pain? We should go."

So, I dropped what I was doing, and guided her quickly out of the store, knocking over the pyramid of apples and creating a huge mess, but there was no time to worry about that. My assumption, like in the movies, is that there was a cab racing by that I could jump in front of and then say something manly like, "GET US TO THE HOSPITAL!" Alas, there was no taxi, so we settled for my car. The bags already had been packed and stored in the back of the car, just in case this emergency landed on us.

The race was on.

We live in the suburbs, about 15 miles west of the hospital that is located in Boston. For some odd reason, there was a lot of traffic at that time of day (an accident up ahead I assumed). Danyael started in with that heavy Lamaze breathing technique . . . do it with me . . . hoo hoo hee, hoo hoo hee. I'm breathing along with her . . . hoo hoo hee, hoo hoo hee.

"How far apart are the contractions?"

"I don't know, four minutes maybEEEEE."

"Hoo hoo hee, hoo hoo hee."

I swerved around cars, speeding (as safely as possible) and zig-zagging like I'm Mario Andretti. I'm somewhat of a nerd so in the recesses of my mind, I'd probably look back at this and feel like I was starring in my own action movie. People are giving me dirty looks as I go past them as I work out how the newscasters will be talking about me on live TV while they show the view from the helicopters and the police cars chasing me down the highway: "Crazy nerd driving erratically toward Boston." They would interview my neighbors and find out that I was always such a nice guy.

"How far apart now? Do you need to squeeze my hand?"

"Groan, I don't know, 3 minuARRRRRGGG."

We eventually arrived at the hospital. I pulled up to the curb, possibly one or two of my wheels literally up on the curb—and I jumped out, left my door open, and ran around the front of the car to my wife's side. Along the way, I contemplated completing the movie arrival by jumping over the hood with that slide technique and also tossing my car keys to some random person walking by and saying something cool like, "Keep it."

I get Danyael into the hospital, she's holding her belly, telling me she needs to start pushing. I say, "*No, don't push, this floor isn't sterilized OR comfortable.*" I think a little joke here and there can only ease the stress of the situation. I am definitely alone in this thinking. Miracle upon miracle, we—with the help of a hospital attendant—got up to the right place and set up for go-time. My wife asked for *the pain drugs* and we got the typical, "*There's no time honey, that baby is coming out either way, right now,*" from a doctor. So, we're all set up and ready to go. My fingers are blue because she's squeezing them so hard (Danyael, not the doctor).

The grunting and groaning, and yelling and screaming, and name-calling and swearing, and punching me in the face, and the accusations of *how could I do this to her* began. The doctor was doing her best quarterback pose, ready to catch the baby. I refer to it as *the baby* at this point because we didn't know if it was a boy or a girl.

The only thing missing is the dramatic music and the shot of our respective families running into the hospital anxiously waiting to hear the results, my mother still with curlers in her hair and my father wearing his over-50 softball uniform, then realizing they went to the wrong hospital; but all in slow-motion.

Finally, after a few more minutes of pushing and one or two farts (offender shall remain nameless), the baby is born.

We have a daughter.

CHAPTER TWO

What Really Happened—Age 0

Here's what really happened:

"Either I just pissed in my pants or my water just broke."

She did really say that. I followed with something like, *"Really? Are you in labor? Any pain?"* Her answer was *no*, so then I asked, *"Should we keep shopping?"* She said *sure*, so that's what we did. My wife (leaking coolant) and I went on our way shopping, I mean, you need to have groceries in the house for when you bring the baby home. The doctor had told us that if the water breaks, as long as there aren't any contractions, that we should just sit tight, but that we should call. Apparently, for risk of infection, they don't want you to go too long with water broken.

We finished our shopping sort of quietly as we both tried to fully grasp what was actually happening, and then headed home. Thankfully, now when I get Fruit Roll-Ups, I can definitely say they aren't for me because everyone knows newborn babies love Fruit Roll-Ups. She called the doctor to let them know that the eagle was landing. *"Okay, sit tight. If you don't feel any pain or contractions by the morning, give a call, we'll want you to come in and get things moving.*" Swell, we'll just sit here all day wondering. We're a bit superstitious so we didn't tell anyone. We also didn't know the sex of the baby, so the excitement and nerves kept building.

We stared at the walls for a while at home, tried to stay calm, checked, double-checked, and triple-checked that everything was ready. I tightened the car seat base a few dozen times.

Nothing.

We were getting into the early evening now. My sister called to tell me that she and my brother-in-law were out for the night and thought they would stop by and say hello. This was literally in the bottom three things that Danyael and I wanted right then. My sister was excited because she suspected, rightfully so, that the baby was coming soon and she just can't get enough of it (her daughter was one year old at the time). We hadn't told them that the train was moving or that we weren't particularly in the mood to hang out.

Naturally, I said, "*Sure, come on over.*"

Danyael and I decided that she would stay in bed and I would say that she wasn't feeling well. Surely, the visit would blow over quickly. Three hours later, my sister, her husband, and I were still down in our basement playing Wii Sports while Danyael was two levels up, watching reruns of "The Gilmore Girls" while waiting to go into active labor. Lord knows, you can never fake Wii bowl enough while waiting for your first child to be born. They left . . . finally.

Still no change. We called the hospital to *check-in* and they told us to just come in first thing in the morning unless something changed overnight. Nothing changed except Danyael, who managed to comfortably fall asleep. I decided I'd prefer to stare at the ceiling all night.

First thing in the morning finally arrived and we got our stuff together and hit the road. Unlike the version that played out in my head, there was literally no traffic because it was Easter Sunday and it was 6:30 in the morning. We took a casual drive to the hospital, parked (ourselves), and casually checked in. On the way in, we did start making the obligatory phone calls. Danyael hales from New York, so her parents had a good drive ahead of them and we wanted them to get here in time. The drive would probably take most people three or four hours, so for them, we knew it would take just under two hours. We thought that might be cutting it close.

About 17 hours and 20 gallons of Pitocin (the drug that gets the contractions moving) later, the fun began. The nurse told me that I was to hold one of Danyael's legs and a hand and also, whisper sweet nothings into her ear (something I'm super uncomfortable even writing)—offering encouragement and an occasional joke. Three hours of that and I devolved to "*Knock knock? Who's there? Interrupting cow. Interrupting cow . . . [mooooo].*"

They decided that it was time for one brave last push before they had to do a C-section. They asked if we wanted them to use the vacuum (to suck the baby out, apparently). I imagined it as a Hoover-looking device, but it wasn't. It turned out, the *vacuum* is a suction cup that they put on top of the head to help guide the baby out.

One seemingly hour-long push, a vacuum suction cupped to the baby's head, lots of squeezing, and one or two farts (offender shall remain nameless) later, our daughter popped out. I didn't even faint—twice.

Julianna was born at 2:36 a.m. on Monday, March 24, 2008.

CHAPTER THREE

About Me

Please don't call me Matthew. Ever.

I can count on one hand how many people do that. I have no objection to the name. I just never felt it suited my personality. Let me tell you a bit about myself and then, I promise, we'll get back to the stuff about the kids. As I travel through parenthood, I find lots of moments when things my kids do remind me of myself or of things that I experienced when I was growing up. I think it might be helpful to have some of that context before we get too much further.

I was born in 1977. I am 46 at the time I'm writing this and have been a proud nerd for the last 40-something years. I was born on my mother's birthday, making me the best gift a mother (Beverly) could get, or so I thought. I grew up with a sister who is three years older than I am (Corey), in a city roughly 13 miles north of Boston. We moved about six houses down the street when I was too young to remember moving. That house was where this nerd was cultivated.

This next part is difficult to believe for people who know me now but didn't know me then: *I was a pretty good athlete*. I was a Little League baseball all-star center fielder. I've been told by a totally unbiased aunt (Marcia) that I could have gone pro had I stuck with it. I played a ton of basketball. I was a varsity tennis player in high school. I really loved sports (and still do)—both playing and watching. Being a rabid Boston sports fan is not that difficult when you've lived your whole life there.

At the same time as playing all the sports, I also was actively exercising my imagination. I loved playing with Star Wars toys, LEGO, G.I. Joe, and Transformers. I was busy deconstructing things in my house (like the time I infamously maybe took the railing off the front steps). I've always enjoyed seeing how things came apart and went back together—how things worked.

The first time I had a girlfriend was in the fifth grade. I believe it was an arranged relationship and while it may be difficult to believe, it didn't last long. Teresa, if you're reading this, I'm sorry I never spoke to you, held your hand, or acknowledged you in any way. It wasn't my fault. Someone told me that you were to be my girlfriend and I went with it. If it makes you feel better, I vaguely remember being told that you were one of the coolest people at the John E. Burke Elementary School.

I had a great core group of friends all the way through high school and traveled in a variety of different social groups. Looking back, I certainly had some run-ins with people who I'd say were bullies, but for the most part, people were good to me.

I was always the shortest one (I'm six-foot-one now, but didn't really grow until my senior year of high school). In my freshman year, I ran for—and won in a landslide—class treasurer. Four years of that set me up for what would be a very long, foreshadowed moment when I would turn 40. It also set me up to be part of organizing every high school reunion for all of eternity (which wasn't in the original job description).

I loved musical theater; not being *in* the productions but rather, working on the tech crew. I participated in as many shows as possible. In the sixth grade, I worked the spotlight for a production of "Barnum" at my middle school. The role of Bailey (as in Barnum & Bailey) was played by a kid (named Corey—but not my sister) whom I wouldn't really become friends with until our senior year of high school. This same person would go on to be my college roommate and the best man at my wedding.

Other than the Teresa situation in the fifth grade, I led a pretty private personal life (read: no long-term girlfriends) all the way until my now-wife (Danyael) and I got engaged. As a result, I'm fairly certain that many people in my life wouldn't have been surprised if I was gay.

Summer camp was a huge part of my life. It became so when I was 10 and has been there ever since. The overnight camp I went to as a kid is the same place where I went on to be a counselor, an administrator, and ultimately, the director. It is where I met my wife. It is the place where both of our daughters currently attend each summer. It is the place where I learned the most about being independent, being a good friend, and being a good person.

I took the SATs for the first time when I was in seventh grade (nerd). I loved school and learning in general (still do). I was 100 percent convinced I would be an architect after college, which was a huge part of deciding to go to Syracuse University (my sister was a senior when I was a freshman, so that helped, too). My plan was to get into Arts & Sciences and then transfer into the School of Architecture.

I never became an architect.

After arriving at Syracuse University, I learned of a new type of program called *Information Studies*.

Before I ever set foot in the School of Architecture, a friend of my sister's told me about this other program called *Information Management and Technology*. It was the single undergraduate major in a tiny new school (under 100 students in the large university). I describe it now as: "Business without the suit and computer science without the pocket protector."

I went to see what the program was all about, met a graduate student who showed me around, and then filled out the transfer paperwork before I left the building. This was the mid-'90s and the modern internet was just being born. I had been tinkering in my dorm room with my own website and was really into how it all worked. This program was perfect for me. I never looked back.

After college, I went on to work for my first software startup (which I had interned with during college) as a software engineer, went through my first sale of company stock to the public and acquisition, experienced the original dot-com bubble burst, and validated that I was in the right career. I would find ways (between startups) to go back to camp for the summer and eventually decided to take a break from the startup life and become the director of that camp.

My first summer as director was when Julianna was a 1-year-old and Chloe, who you've yet to meet, was 3 months old. Those were tough years. After two years of being the director and not feeling great about my relationships with my daughters, I decided to go back to the startup world, and that's where I've been ever since.

Now, I'm married with a wife, two daughters, a cat, two dogs, two axolotls (look it up—trust me), and about forty fish divided across two tanks. We live in the suburbs, about 13 miles west of Boston. I started writing a dad blog years ago (which ultimately led to this). I try to be as involved with my daughters' lives as I can and as involved in the town as possible. In the winter of 2018, I ran for, and won a seat on our town's School Committee (in Massachusetts, we like to do things our own way so we don't call it a School Board).

And that is where we are and that is my story in a chapter-long nutshell.

CHAPTER FOUR

Parenting DNA

I wanted to go through an exercise and explore the various influences that have contributed to what I'd refer to as my *Parenting DNA*. I wouldn't be able to reasonably and objectively correlate any of this directly, but I do think it's worth acknowledging some of the people and experiences that I think have affected the way I parent.

I've already spoken about my background a bit and now I'll zoom in a little and get a bit more specific. My mother likes to tell me that I'm *anal-retentive*, but I like to think of it as *hyper-observant*. As a result, I have always enjoyed learning from the people and the things going on around me.

My parents, Bev and Lenny, were (and are) a huge part of my life. Both of my parents were very involved in my childhood, but in different ways. My sense of humor, for instance, definitely comes from my mother's side. We not only share a birthday (she's way older though; like . . . WAY older) but also share an immunity to public embarrassment attempts or the concept of shame. If I told you her maiden name is *Penis* you'd think I was joking; and I am. Her maiden name is *Dick*. When you grow up with that last name, you are required to have a thick skin and a robust sense of humor. Her mother, Phyllis Dick (let that sit for a second), is where she got her sense of humor.

I remember coming home from school as a child and getting a snack, which was usually a Drake's Coffee Cake pack of two. There were occasionally problems with this snack choice because sometimes my dad would have one of the cakes and put the open package back in the box, which everyone knows is a full-on psycho move because the cake, once exposed to oxygen, has about eight minutes of life before it becomes a piece of granite. Anyhow, I'd get my snack and then sit with my mother to watch her favorite soap opera—"General Hospital." For many years, I was enthralled with the Luke and Laura storyline or what kind of nefarious plot Sonny Corinthos was cooking up. The good news is, once we had enough of GH (which is what we fans of the fictional city of Port Charles called it), we settled into episodes of "The Golden Girls."

To this day, "The Golden Girls" remains one of my all-time favorite shows. Dorothy, Rose, Blanche, and Sophia made me laugh my ass off every episode. Since I got married, I've been trying to name a pet—any pet—after one of the girls. I fought to name our first dog Blanche. I lost. One day.

My mom and I did puzzles together, played card games, and spent a lot of time laughing.

When I was in the third grade, I got chicken pox. I remember being home from school, laying in my parent's bed watching TV (probably "The Price is Right"), and my dad walking into the room with two toys. He told me that I could choose one of the toys with a smile on his face. I chose both. He has always been that sort of person—buy something for someone, for no particular reason, because it makes them happy. Not too long ago, one of the daughters of a family friend of ours who is in second grade had to be home from school because she had COVID. She was bored out of her mind (I assume) and was sending me chat messages via Facebook Messenger Kids. We did a video chat and spoke for around 30 minutes. I asked her about her favorite things to play with or books to read. We had a lovely discussion. As soon as we *hung up* I went to the store and got her some Pokemon cards, a LEGO Friends set, and the next two books in the series she was reading. I dropped off a bag of stuff on her front steps and shortly thereafter got the cutest thank you video message I've ever gotten.

My dad and I also spent a lot of time bonding over sports. Between his participation in men's basketball and softball leagues along with my participation in a kids' basketball league, Little League baseball (my aunt once told me that she thought I could have gone pro—which I believe to be true), and varsity tennis in high school, there was a lot of time spent in the world of sports.

My first summer at summer camp was a doozy. I was 10 years old (a bit of a late start—retrospectively ironic). I had never spent any significant time away from home or my parents. As part of the camp program, there were day trips out of camp. One of these—the first I ever went on with camp—was to a place called "Water Country" in Portsmouth, N.H.

> WATER COUNTRY
> "When the sun is blazing and the summer gets hot . . .
> Water Country is a very cool spot.
> There's no better place to feel beyond.
> Water Country have some fun!
> Water Country, Water Country, Water Country, have
>   some fun!"

While that was the jingle, it was not, unfortunately, how my first experience went. For trips out of camp, the campers are split into groups and assigned to a group leader. These days, that leader is always a counselor but back then, it could have been—and was for me—a counselor-in-training (CIT). See, I was not much of a swimmer or much of an adventure ride person. This made *Water Country* more like *No Thank You Country*. It is worth noting that at the end of my career as a camper, I did receive a Participation Trophy from the swimming department for five summers of standing ankle-deep in the lake.

The kids in my group decided they wanted to go down the largest water slide in the park, which, given my short stature at the time, I think was probably like 500 feet tall (note: I looked it up: 58 feet). Anyhow, I didn't want to go. My CIT, Ben, told me to wait at the bottom of the slide and they'd be right down. I stood there, holding the railing where people got off the slide, and watched as my group walked to the line to go up to the top.

It is worth noting, what might ultimately seem obvious: on trips outside of camp, for safety reasons, everyone wears T-shirts that have the camp name on them. Counselors have different colored shirts so they can be easily seen. Given Water Country's nature, nobody was wearing a camp T-shirt. Everyone was wearing no shirt. This made it quite challenging for me, particularly as a new camper who knew very few people, to identify anyone from camp.

So, I stood at the bottom of the slide and waited.

And waited.

And waited.

Each *and waited* caused me to grip the railing a little bit tighter. You know that feeling in the pit of your stomach when you start to sense that something is wrong? It slowly crawls up in you. You start by telling yourself to just be patient; everything is fine. Even when you start to see evidence that things aren't fine, like when you notice that someone who went up to the top of the slide after your group has since come down, you tell yourself ridiculous things like, "Maybe someone in my group had to tie their shoes and let people cut the line," even though your rational brain reminds you that nobody is wearing shoes.

And waited.

At this point, I thought I had no more blood in my fingers because I was gripping the railing so tightly. Eventually, a different counselor walked by and saw me standing there like a ghost. I didn't have a mirror on me, but I imagine I looked very upset (probably because I was). He had me stay with him and his group for the rest of the trip. I was saved.

What ended up happening was that my group went up the stairs and decided that the line was too long. The same stairs also led to a different set of slides that came down in a different area. They went down those slides and forgot to come get me. They had long since left the area, and me. For the record, that CIT, Ben, is someone I am still friends with. He went on to be one of my favorite counselors (three different summers), so while I am capable of forgiveness, I certainly never forgot that moment. That moment, as traumatic as it was for me, certainly affected how I was as a counselor and I think how I am as a parent. In subsequent visits to Water Country for many years (as a camper and then as a counselor), each time I walked by that spot, I could still *feel* how I felt back in 1988. I could practically see dents in the railing where I had been holding on.

As a counselor, then as a head counselor, and ultimately as the director of the camp, I prided myself on the attention paid to each of my campers and on really getting to know them and making sure they felt safe. Again, my first experience at Water Country was quite awful but for Ben the CIT, it was an innocent mistake that we laugh about now. For me, it certainly played a huge part in the way I pay attention to what's going on around me and in particular, as a parent.

And then there was Danyael. I'll talk more about her and our story later but for now, I'll say this: it wasn't until after she and I started dating that I figured out I had always struggled with confidence. While I knew I was pretty good at my job, I was never great with relationships. I never felt comfortable interacting socially or being comfortable in my own skin. As we were dating, and then ultimately got engaged and married, she taught me that it was okay to be myself. Growing up, I never felt like I was cool. Here is someone, Danyael, who was cool with showing me that all my quarks and nerdy things are fine. I think my sense of humor—and yes, massive intelligence—perhaps masked my lack of confidence. Now, I have a much greater sense of confidence in things beyond my professional work. This confidence is a central theme for me as a parent and for our daughters in their development. I wouldn't have that tool without Danyael.

I also wouldn't have kids without Danyael, so. . . .

I guess one way to imagine parenting, or rather, one way *I* imagined parenting, is using the concept that a lot of video games use—the fog of war. You know you are on some sort of map but you can't see very much of it. Most of the map is covered in a fog. It isn't until you start traveling across the map that the fog dissipates. Unlike in video games, there is no cheat code to clear the fog of war when you are a parent. You just have to experience it and figure it out as you go. Those are just some of the people and experiences that helped give me the tools to travel across that map.

CHAPTER FIVE

Sibling—Age 0

"Did you just get pregnant again?"

That isn't possible, right? You can't get pregnant just about three months after you just brought home a newborn, right? If not biologically, there must be some magical reason that doesn't happen.

Well, it turns out, one can get pregnant three months after just bringing home a newborn baby.

3. Fucking. Months. Later.

Well, I guess we're doing this. My wife and I always knew we wanted to have kids and get to it pretty quickly. We got married in 2007. Julianna was born in 2008 and now we were on schedule for another member of the family in 2009. While Julianna had been born in March of 2008, this next one was due in April of 2009.

So, there we were, three months into our brand-new adventure as parents, maybe starting to scratch the surface of how to do the job and my wife was pregnant again. I think we thought, "There's no way it's going to happen that quickly, so we might

21

as well get started." For so many people, it can take quite a bit of time to get pregnant—if a couple can do it at all. We were very lucky with Julianna and even luckier this time.

When my wife and I started dating, she was living in New York City and I was in Boston. We would see each other every other weekend. We alternated between me going to NYC and her coming to Boston. We did this for nine months before we got engaged in May of 2006. We were married—you guessed it—nine months later. Three months after we got married, she got pregnant and now we found ourselves in the same situation again.

No rest for the weary.

When we got married, we clearly didn't spend a ton of time just being married—alone with each other—before Julianna entered the picture. Now, we were not going to spend a lot of time with just Julianna before we forced her to share another baby with us.

One of the bright sides, we told ourselves, was that she was going to be a sister a lot sooner than we had thought. This was by no means an accident. It was quite the opposite in fact. I'd be lying if I said it didn't scare the shit out of me, though. How were we going to manage two little humans? I suppose we were about to find out.

Like with Julianna, we did not find out the sex of the baby ahead of time, although, we did consider it a little longer than the first time. It felt more practical this time around. We had all this baby girl stuff and it would have been helpful to know if we could donate or get rid of stuff Julianna had outgrown or if we should hold on to it. My wife also got an amniocentesis this time around. This is the test where the doctor sticks a five-inch needle into the pregnant woman's uterus to get a sample of amniotic fluid, or something. This fluid is used to test for developmental abnormalities in the fetus . . . and can determine the gender of the baby.

We were not going to do anything about the pregnancy if the results were bad. We just felt like if they were bad, we could use the time to be prepared for what was ahead, especially now because we had another child in the family. The results were normal and the pregnancy was relatively normal (easy for me to say). The one big difference this time around was that with our first daughter, my wife was considered *high risk* which at the time, was the case because Danyael was turning 35 years old during that pregnancy and it was her first. As a result, we got to see ultrasounds pretty much monthly at the beginning and weekly toward the end.

Remember that my college major was *information management*. Being able to get so many good looks at our baby was incredibly comforting. This time around, she was not considered high risk, so we only had the ultrasound toward the beginning of the pregnancy and then not again until toward the end. We were in the relative dark for most of this go-round.

We powered through (my wife, obviously, more than I). We practiced our diaper-changing skills and swaddling on a real person rather than an old Cabbage Patch Kid. We bought a second set of baby furniture, moved Julianna over to a new bedroom, and reset the nursery.

As the morning of April 13, 2009, rolled around, Julianna was almost but not quite 13 months old, and Danyael's water broke. Similar to our experience with Julianna, there was no exciting or emergency labor situation. Dissimilar to Julianna, there was also no 36-hour marathon. Danyael felt no pain or contractions and the requisite call to the obstetrician went as expected: "*Come on into the hospital.*"

We called my sister (you remember—the one whom we misled for hours the last time this happened while my wife rested in bed and I played video games) and asked her to come and watch Julianna because we had to go into the hospital. Fun fact: she also was pregnant at the time and would give birth to her second child—a son—five weeks later. To this day, her son and this baby who was about to be born are like an old married couple. My sister also had a now two-year-old toddler at home.

In we went. We got into the triage room (last curtain on the right) and sat patiently. Given the baby situation at home, I think we were both happy to sit in a relatively quiet place for some downtime.

Another fun fact: April 13, 2009, was the day after Easter. March 24, 2008—the day Julianna was born—was also the day after Easter. That might have been meaningful to us if not for the fact that we're Jewish.

My wife was checked and it was determined that we were not going home without a birth happening first. We waited in the curtain area until it was time to move to a labor and delivery room. These types of triage rooms are funny places. You don't really see any other people but you hear lots of discussions. All these people are here for the same reason—get that baby.

I remember feeling a sense of brotherhood/dating game with all the people in the ward, even if we never met or knew what the others looked like. We were all going through similar situations. Some of us would be sent home, some to a private room, but soon, we would all be experiencing some sort of *family moment*.

We had some time to sit there and wait as the nerves started to ramp up with no TV to distract us (and trepidation to talk to each other because it didn't feel at all private). As a matter of fact, you could almost feel the similar sentiments from the other people who were going through the same experience. There was no entertainment but for this one asshole. By my sound projection skills, I'd put him at around three curtains down and across the aisle. He and his partner (I don't know if they were married) were there for their first child, but that didn't stop him from flirting with their assigned nurse. When they were told it wasn't time for them and they should go home, his response, loudly, was, "Awesome. Who wants to be born on the 13th anyway? It's bad luck." I imagine a good handful of us—within our various curtains—were all collectively rolling our eyes while holding our middle fingers up pointing in his general direction.

We were moved into a private labor and delivery room shortly after. The bed was on the opposite wall this time which totally threw me off. As opposed to the last time, with Julianna, this time, things seemed like they were moving relatively quickly. It was also the middle of the day as opposed to the middle of the night. Things were lining up nicely.

As is fairly common with a second child, the active labor segment of the festivities is typically faster than with the first. It was this way for us. With me holding one of her legs, like I had with Julianna, my wife started to push around 2 p.m.

No farting this time. At 2:16, I watched the birth of my second child. Like with Julianna, it took what my wife thought was an hour but was actually a few seconds for me to communicate to her what the biological structure was between this baby's legs.

It was a vagina.

Chloe was born.

CHAPTER SIX

Job #1

At some point in my career, I started thinking about the things that were actually important to me—the things that made it fun and interesting to get up and go to work each day. These things have changed for me as my career has evolved, which makes perfect sense, given that my life also has changed.

If I was to look back on the earlier days of my career—when I was a single guy with no children and really nobody to worry about other than myself—the things that were important to me went something like this:

- Work on a project that is really interesting
- Work with people whom I can learn from
- Get paid (ideally, a lot of money)
- Have stock options (this was before the first dot-com bubble burst in the early 2000s)

For quite a while, these things didn't change all that much for me. They might have gotten a bit more specific (like working with particular technologies) but in general, as long as it was just me, these important things were *the* important things.

Whenever I conduct a job interview these days, I like to ask people a question related to this, in order to get an idea of what's important to them. It is always—truly—judgement free and usually, it is very informative. For example, if what's important to a candidate is that they get a company car, and our company doesn't do that, it is important that we are aligned in our understanding that this just isn't a good fit.

And so, my important things were very much normal and self-centered—reasonably, in my opinion—until Julianna was born. Once that happened, there was a shift. To be clear, I'm no superhero when it comes to this sort of thing. I'm fairly certain that most parents, once they become parents, reprioritize their lives. The problem was that I wasn't really aware of all this *what's really important to me stuff* at the time. I knew that I liked being happy when I went to work more than I liked being miserable or bored, but again, that makes me just like everyone else.

Prior to having kids, I always had one job—the professional one. Now I had two jobs and had to figure out a way to make sure that they were properly prioritized. More importantly, what I didn't know then but I do know now, is that the concept of work/life balance that is so often spoken of—in the context of the startup technology space, for me—is bullshit. There is no balance with work and life. They aren't on either side of a seesaw but rather intertwined like a French braid. Success or failure in one can deeply affect your probability of being a success or a failure in the other. This might not be the case for you, but it was and certainly still is the case for me.

When I took the job as the full-time director of the summer camp where I grew up and met my wife, it felt like a dream job. Camp had been such a special place for me as a kid. When I had the opportunity to become a counselor there, it was an incredible experience; I got to give back what was hopefully a similar experience for the campers in my cabin. When I got the opportunity to be the head counselor for all of the boys, it was the same benefit, but this time for 150 kids rather than 12. When I became the assistant program director, I was helping in some small way to make camp awesome for all 350 kids.

Finally, when I became the director, which is a full-time, year-round job, I was charged with not only making camp incredible for all 350 kids, but also with creating a great experience for all of their parents as well as the 100-plus staff members. I got to take kids and their families around camp on tours and show them the same magic that I saw. It was an incredible job and an incredible experience.

But there was a problem. For nine months each year, it was a fairly normal job with an average amount of travel and some weekend work (going to camp fairs and conferences). There were some night calls with parents (when it was convenient for them to talk after work). For the other three months, June through August, I moved up to the camp in New Hampshire. There is a director's cabin with two small bedrooms, a small bathroom with a stall shower, and an even smaller kitchenette. In certain circumstances, this would have been great.

I started as the director in September of 2008. This was right after the summer session had finished and would give me a full cycle to prepare. Julianna was five months old (and my wife was two months pregnant). I didn't move up to camp until June of 2009. In between those times, my wife gave birth; Julianna was now just over a year old and Chloe was three months old. My wife had a job and had just gone back to work. She worked from home which was a benefit, but having a newborn and a just-toddler is a lot to take on with me essentially moving away for three months to do a job that for all intents and purposes requires my attention 24/7.

Our arrangement was that my wife would drive up to camp—a little more than an hour north of where we lived—on Thursday nights (she wasn't working on Fridays at the time) with the mini-van stuffed with car seats, babies, bottles, toys, diapers, and a whole lot of potential stress. I was always so excited when they would arrive, but was also constantly being pulled in a thousand directions for the job. I would put the Baby Bjorn on and throw Chloe in there and walk around camp. I was trying to find any way to help while still making sure I was doing my duty for all the people at camp.

This was a very difficult time for us. Babies, as you might know, are unpredictable. Chloe had stomach and constipation problems from a young age which led to a lot of crying and a lot of needing to be held. My wife had a lot of earned stress as a result, which led to a lot of crying and a lot of needing to be held. I started feeling like I wasn't being a supportive husband or a good father and I wasn't building a nice relationship with my kids, particularly Chloe. I was missing *first moments* that were happening during the summer—like when Julianna took her first steps *at camp* with my wife and one of the other camp administrators (thanks a lot, DAN).

We survived the first summer and things settled down as the new session-planning started. By the time the following June rolled around, we were all a bit better at things. Julianna was now just over two years old and Chloe was just over one. She still had the stomach issues and still needed to be held all the time, but at least my wife and I had another year of parenting experience and I had another year of camp director experience. We had a better idea of how to do the camp visits. Things would surely be better.

They weren't. It was really more of the same except now, the kids could actually, sort of, communicate that they wanted to spend time with me but my schedule and work responsibilities didn't allow it. Regularly, I would sneak away around 7 p.m.—their bedtime—when they were visiting, so I could be with them. Unfortunately, 7 p.m. at camp is *free play* time, and the time that people are getting ready for that night's evening activities. More often than I'd care to admit, I'd be sitting on the floor in the tiny second bedroom, which at this point held two cribs, reading "Goodnight Moon" and trying to have some small sliver of quiet time with my girls when someone would knock on the door and need something from me.

These were always difficult moments because even if there was someone who would have been a fine alternative to me to take care of whatever the problem was, it was always my responsibility to deal with it. Regardless, the knock on the door would break up the moment I was having with my kids.

Toward the end of that summer, I remember a conversation I had with my wife just before the camp summer ended in which I told her that I was done. I loved that job and I continue to love camp and stay involved in whatever ways I can to this day. I was also fortunate enough to have a very different passion and skill set in software development. I knew that I could return to the startup tech space and not have to be away from my family or put them in this kind of stressful situation for three months a year.

I felt like Chloe didn't know me; that she felt no connection with me. Julianna was a bit older and seemed to have a better understanding of where I was and what I was doing.

The summer ended and I resigned shortly after. I went back to work in the tech space and have been there ever since.

The thing that became abundantly clear during those two years was that I would no longer try to find a compromise between my professional job and my job as a parent. My responsibility was to be present for my family. My kids would always come first. Since that time, during job interviews, I am always upfront about my intention to be a parent first. I'm sure this has eliminated me from consideration for certain jobs, but it's just not something I'm flexible about.

I try very hard to be home for dinner each night and to spend as much time with my daughters as I can. They won't always want to spend time with me, but for as long as they want me around, I want to be there.

The result of this has been that I feel like I'm doing a better job as a parent and am, therefore, not staring at the ceiling all night feeling guilty about going to work the next day. Because I feel better about the job I'm doing as a parent, I'm happier to go to work at companies who also agree that being a parent is my primary job. Because I'm happier going to work each day, the quality of said work makes the company happy and more willing to tolerate me leaving early enough to get home for dinner. Because the company is supportive of me leaving early enough to get home for dinner with my family, I also am more willing to get back online—and do more work—after the girls go to bed at night.

It is cyclical and all part of one thing. There is nothing to balance.

What is important to you?

CHAPTER SEVEN

The Bedtime Routine—Ages 0–5

Danyael is somewhat of a Microsoft Excel whiz. She loves a good spreadsheet. Her job involves business management and accounting work. She is very well-organized and enjoys structure. Given that I am a software engineer by trade, it should probably not be much of a surprise that I enjoy a good routine and also enjoy being organized and planning things out.

Both Julianna and Chloe were outstanding sleepers, from very early on. While, scientifically speaking, it would be challenging to attribute their high-quality sleeping skills to the bedtime routine we implemented for both of them, you can't rule it out.

When they were babies, we adhered to the following routine every night, and had great success. There might be no better feeling as a new parent than when you put your baby in the crib, slowly tip-toe out of the room like a cartoon cat burglar, give yourself a solid 45 seconds to close the door so slowly that you fear it will be dawn before you've fully closed it, and then slowly take your hand off the knob safely outside the room—all with a baby who is not crying.

Start the routine at or around the same time every night.

My wife and I would divide and conquer. She'd go with one daughter and I'd go with the other. We would alternate each night. Into the rooms we'd go, closing the door so we would be distraction free. I can only assume my wife was doing the same routine as I was:

1. *Prep*: Lights on at their normal brightness. A bottle ready next to the chair. We would go pick out a book to read. This part is critical: We are not doing a diaper change to start. We didn't have a white noise machine in their rooms but we did have old iPods and each had playlists of just white noise types of sounds like a clothes dryer or rainfall. The playlist was the same three or four sound *songs* and we'd add each a bunch of times to create a multi-hour extravaganza of noise. We pressed *play* on the list, but the volume was barely audible.

2. *Off to the chair to read a book*: Perhaps we will read "Jamberry" or maybe tonight is "Goodnight Moon." Reading was such an essential part of our routine and something my wife and I thought was so important. Both girls really loved being read to and we loved doing it.

3. *Once the book was finished it was time to start the bottle*: The room was quiet and relaxing. After around a quarter of the bottle was finished, it was time for the magic. We dim the lights a bit and turn the white noise playlist up a bit louder—another quarter of the bottle, a bit dimmer on the lights, and a bit louder on the playlist. After we have gotten three quarters of the way through the bottle it was time for a diaper change and to get into our sleep sack/swaddle situation. At this point, relaxation set in quite nicely for all of us. The house was getting quieter and everyone was calm.

4. *From here, we would go back to the glider chair, feeling nice and clean with a dry diaper and a warm swaddle (the babies—not the parents—just to be clear)*: The lights were very dim now and the white noise was loud enough to be white noise. Whichever daughter I was with would finish the bottle and have a few good burps, then we would sit in the chair, rocking gently and letting ourselves feel very relaxed. You're getting sleepy just reading this, and NOT because you're bored.

5. This is the critical part: Do not let that baby fall asleep in your arms. Just before that happens, while she is calm, full, and clean, but still awake (barely), you place her into the crib. You can see it in her eyes. It's that feeling you have when you're exhausted and can't wait to put your head on your pillow. When it happens, you almost immediately fall asleep.

By putting them in the crib while they were still awake, they regarded the crib as a place that is relaxing and comfortable. More often than not, they'd be fast asleep before the 45 seconds it took to close the door.

This was the routine for as long as they were drinking bottles. Every night.

Once they got a bit older and moved out of cribs, the routine changed. The emphasis then was still to help them slowly relax and *bring their energy level down*, but at that point, we focused more on reading. As they got older and more autonomous, they would go to their respective bookshelves and choose a book or two that they'd like to have read to them. My wife and I would each get into the bed of whomever our turn was that night and read to them. I really loved this phase. I have always enjoyed reading and always wanted my daughters to love reading, too. But bedtime was special because there were no screens or distractions—just me and one of my daughters reading a nice book and recapping the day. The lights would still be a little dim and the room would be warm.

I vividly remember these nights of just being in the bed with them and at least partially wishing that they could stay that age forever. These were the times when you'd finish a book and get the "one more book, Daddy" plea. How could I resist? Of course, we're going to read one more book.

There were even times in this phase when they would fall asleep while I was reading. This was the worst. It meant I had to figure out a way to get out of the bed, navigating the sea of 1000 stuffed animals, and not make any noise or too much movement that might disturb them.

This was also a great time, when they were a bit older, to talk about not only the day we just had, but to talk about whatever fun things were going to happen tomorrow. Both Julianna and Chloe, although a bit more from the latter, would get anxious about any sort of change or mystery that they knew was coming up. Talking about it in advance was always a good way to take the edge off by removing some of the mystery. Any mitigation of tomorrow's anxiety that we could do tonight was a win. It's a tightrope: I never wanted to introduce any additional anxiety or awaken any anxiety that might not be at the top of either of their minds, but . . . if I could identify something that might be simmering in one of their heads and lower the temperature before it got to a boil, that was a victory.

For example, Chloe used to get very nervous about thunder and lightning. To her, it was unpredictable and occasionally loud—and that can be scary (like it is for many people and quite a few pets). One day, I decided to try something when some thunder started quietly rumbling in the distance. I took out my phone and opened a weather app. Inside the app, I went to the map that showed the weather traveling through time. I explained to her that the little blue dot in the middle was *us* and then showed her the clouds and how the different colors represented different types of weather. We zoomed in and looked at where the rain was and how the orange and red areas were thunder and lightning. Because we could slide *time* around and watch the animation, we could see exactly when the thunder would be passing over our house and how long it would last. It turns out that this took the bite out of the problem because now we weren't talking about some mystery lights and sounds coming from the sky at random intervals. Now, thunder and lightning was just another part of the schedule that would last for another 15 minutes (or whatever the app showed us). It immediately calmed her down.

From then on, any time she would hear a little thunder or see a flash of lightning, she would ask me to show her the weather map. While she still didn't LOVE the intense weather, it didn't bother her nearly as much now that we made it more *predictable*.

It feels like forever ago that this was the nightly routine. Now, the nightly routine is this:

> DAUGHTER: "Dad, can you get me some water and a snack?"
>
> ME: "No. Get it yourself. I'm going to sleep."
>
> DAUGHTER: "K. I'll be up for a while."
>
> ME: "Any chance you want to come read me a book?"
>
> DAUGHTER: [crickets]

PART II

Relationships

CHAPTER EIGHT

Becoming Friends—Ages 1–4

At some point during the time when Chloe was around a year and a half old and Julianna was around two and a half, I think they went from just being sisters to also being friends.

They were both going through very different phases of their development and from the very beginning, their personalities couldn't have been more different (but more on that in the next chapter). Danyael and I, from the beginning, wondered what the dynamic would become between the two of them and we were about to find out.

At first, their interactions were pretty basic because Chloe was so young and Julianna was old enough to actually play. Julianna didn't pay much attention to Chloe except for the occasional *make-nice* head smack. On we went. Chloe started trying to move and eventually got up on her feet.

At this point, the chase was on.

There was plenty of *making nice*, but Julianna was treating her sister more like one of her toys rather than another actual person. As Chloe's personality developed into a silly, happy-go-lucky *monsterpiece* of a toddler, Julianna was largely oblivious and continued on her merry way. Julianna, at this point, was enjoying coloring, reading, her baby dolls, and using her imagination. Chloe liked trucking from one side of the room to the other, playing with Elmo, and squatting in corners to facilitate the arrival of hard-earned doodies (she dealt with a lot of constipation issues as a baby/toddler).

Then it started . . .

Chloe started to take an interest in Julianna's activities. Julianna realized she had someone else to talk to, even if that someone couldn't exactly talk back. Then, one day and out of nowhere, the *Hot Dog!* dance came on at the end of the "Mickey Mouse Clubhouse":

> Hot dog, oh no, hot dog
> Hot dog, hot dog, hot diggety dog
> Now we got ears, it's time for cheers
> Hot dog, hot dog, the problem's solved
> Hot dog, hot dog, hot diggety dog
>
> Grab my boots and a sandwich
> Let's start a parade
> Get the coconut drum kit
> For Daisy to play
>
> Hot dog, hot dog, hot diggety dog
> We're taking off, we're dancing now
> Hot dog, leapfrog and holy cow
> Hot dog, hot dog, hot diggety dog
>
> Hot dog, hot dog, hot diggety dog
> It's a brand new day, whatcha waiting for?
> Get up, stretch out, stomp on the floor
> Hot dog, hot dog, hot diggety dog

Hot dog, hot dog, hot diggety dog
We're splitting the scene, we're full of beans
So long for now from Mickey Mouse
And the Mickey Mouse Clubhouse

If your kids ever watched this show, you know it was an opportunity for you to get a few things done around the house. This song, I believe, was actually a signal from Mickey to us parents letting us know it was about to be time to get back on duty.

When the song struck, both girls got up in the living room and started dancing together, laughing with each other, and trying to communicate which dance steps were next. This first time was a realization that they each had a partner in crime.

From that moment on, during car rides, they would often stare at each other and *talk*, make faces at each other, sing together, and even pass toys and books back and forth. Sharing toys and books was a big step but it wasn't for some time after that when Julianna—who had a bag of *Pirate's Booty* popcorn—without any prompting, reached out and gave a handful to Chloe. For me, this is the ultimate sign of friendship—snacks. Sharing a toy is great, but we know that if someone else gets a turn with the toy, you can always get another turn. When you're willing to give up a prized and limited supply possession like a snack, knowing that you won't get that back, it is the true sign of caring for another.

It's hard to know when—and in what form—your kids are going to become friends. I had no timeline, but I think I just assumed it would happen eventually. As a young parent at the time, I told myself I'd be thrilled if they were close friends but would probably have settled for them to *tolerate each other*. I think all parents would all be thrilled if their children were close. It is reasonable to think that there will be ups and downs throughout their respective journeys. I remember thinking that while it is completely unknown what they will be to each other down the road, in that moment, I was witnessing the beginning of something.

My sister (who is WAY older than I am: three years) and I were probably more in the *we tolerate each other* category until after college. Now, we're pretty close and what I would consider also to be good friends. This is perhaps because while growing up I was younger, nerdier, and more annoying. We were also just the right distance apart in years to make it awkward in school. When I was in sixth grade (the first year of middle school where we grew up in Peabody, MA), she was in ninth grade at the high school, so we were in different buildings. When I was in ninth grade, she was in 12th. No senior in high school wants to socialize with a freshman, let alone a freshman who is in the National Honor Society and took (and scored well on) the SATs when he was in seventh grade. So, I get it.

We both also played a lot of sports and that is where most of our interactions originated. We would play tag football in the backyard with our dad. We would play one-on-one basketball in the driveway. Given how undersized I was for my—or any—age, my sister did a lot of dominating on the field and court, until I started being not undersized and then things, I think, were less fun for her.

We even went to the same college—Syracuse University. When I arrived at college, she was a senior and I was a freshman—again. This time, unlike high school, we actually got along well. It is worth noting that I applied to the School of Arts & Sciences at Syracuse but fully intended to transfer to their acclaimed School of Architecture. If not for a fateful dinner invitation that my sister extended to me to join her and some of her friends one night during my first semester, I might not have tripped over a fairly significant fork in the road.

One of her friends told me about this new program called the School of Information Studies. They had one major called

Information Management & Technology. I now describe it as "a combination of business without the suit and computer science without the pocket protector." It sounded interesting and I had been tinkering with—and enjoying—this thing called the *Internet* and the *World Wide Web* in my dorm room, because that's what you do when you go to college and have limited social skills. This was 1995 and the internet as we know it was just beginning. I just meandered into the school the next day (half of the fourth floor of what was called the Sci-Tech Building on the edge of campus). I ran into a student getting his master's degree in the school and he gave me the 10-minute tour (and sales pitch).

In what was probably the most short-sighted and impulsive decision of my life, I walked into the administrative office—without consulting with my parents, any friends, or even my sister—and filled out transfer papers. Architecture Schmarchitecture; I never looked back. The rest is history. I'm not sure if you're familiar with the Internet but it turned into a pretty big thing from there. The School of Information Studies is now called *The iSchool* and has its own building on the quad in the center of campus, with many more students than when I attended.

All of that happened because my sister decided to invite me to dinner with her friends. We all win.

So, back to Julianna and Chloe. At that time, and even today, I can't tell what their future will hold in terms of friendship. They are sometimes oil and water and sometimes peanut butter and jelly. I'm sure that trend will continue for a long time. Friendship is a continuum. Sibling friendship is no different.

Another one of the shows they watched when they were a bit older was called "Liv and Maddie." This is a show where an actress, Dove Cameron, played twin sisters (expertly I'd say, especially for a teeny-bopper-style show). Each of the sisters was very different. One was into sports. The other was into the arts. They dressed differently, spoke differently, had different friends, etc. While Julianna and Chloe aren't twins, they aren't far off and the distinction in personalities between Liv and Maddie is pretty similar as well.

On that show, they had a saying. We took that saying and printed it on a photograph of Julianna and Chloe together in a sunset. The saying has two parts so we made two different framed canvases of the photograph—each with one part of the saying. To this day, one is on Julianna's bedroom door and the other is on Chloe's door:

Sisters by chance.
Friends by choice.

CHAPTER NINE

Cats And Dogs—Ages 2–5

Chloe is like a cat. Julianna is like a dog.

Chloe takes a long time to *warm up* to new people and new situations. She has always been apprehensive and just doesn't trust people easily. When you first meet her, I'm not sure you'd describe her as *warm and fuzzy*. She's also incredibly sharp and cunning and sneaky. The hair on the back of her neck even stands up when she feels threatened. Just like a cat, things happen on Chloe's terms. Once she decides that you are worthy, she is incredibly loyal, never wants to leave your side, and occasionally coughs up a leaf from a plant her mother has on a shelf that you didn't think was possible to reach.

Julianna, on the other hand, is very outgoing and friendly right from the beginning. She's more whimsical and warm and open to trying new things. Among her friends, she is the connector (mostly for better—but not always). Julianna is wonderful at making new friends and at just going along for the ride. She is very intuitive and empathetic and is a total social butterfly. She is also really good at bringing the tennis ball back when I throw it.

Their foundational outlook on interactions with other humans couldn't be further apart.

It is worth noting—for those who are overly sensitive—I don't actually think my daughters are cats or dogs. We actually have a cat (his name is Charlie) and two dogs (Cassie and Annie, both girls) as part of our family. I know the differences between humans, felines, and canines.

This distinction in personalities is something I've spent a lot of time thinking about over the years. In most ways, I think the distinction is a good thing. Because the girls are so close in age, I think anything that makes them very obviously different is helpful. Are there times when I wish Julianna wouldn't be so susceptible to FOMO (fear of missing out)? Sure. Are there times when I wish Chloe would just come downstairs and say *hello* to one of my friends who stopped by? Sure.

Mostly, though, I have a great appreciation for their uniqueness from each other—and Danyael and I try to help them lean into their personalities. It's not always easy to have children who are not quite 13 months apart in age and almost 180 degrees apart in personality.

When Danyael and I got married, we were pretty aligned on trying to have kids quickly. Having no idea how long that process might take, we didn't want to wait. My wife was pregnant with Julianna shortly after we got married. As I mentioned earlier, Julianna was born in March of 2008. While we knew we wanted more kids, we figured that it would—*for sure*—take longer for her to get pregnant the second time around . . . because, you know . . . #science.

In June of 2008, three months after Julianna's birth, it came as a surprise to both of us that Danyael was pregnant again. I won't go through the whole story again, but will focus on one of the things that went through my head in that whirlwind of nine months. Julianna doesn't remember a world without her sister.

She was not quite 13 months old when Chloe was born. In some ways, that's a sneaky advantage to her. She never really reaped the benefits of being an only child from an attention perspective, so she didn't miss it when she all of a sudden had to share her parents with a sibling.

It did cross my mind though that Chloe—because she was so close in age—would spend the entirety of her life chasing just behind Julianna. What if she had all the same interests? What if she had the same sense of style? Liked the same toys? What if she ended up feeling like she's always in the shadow of a slightly older sister who gets to do everything first?

The question I suppose I found myself asking myself was, "How are we going to make sure that both girls grow up in an environment where they can have all the happiness and bickering, love and hatred, silliness and bickering, and sharing and bickering that one gets from having a sibling while also having their own interests—their own personalities?"

What I didn't know then, but do now, is that it was largely out of my control. Kids will be kids. I can't explain it. Fortunately, Chloe did, in fact, have quite a different personality and very different interests. This made the concept of *chasing* her sister slightly less acute. Unfortunately, Chloe, given her cat-like instincts, does have a competitive streak and does occasionally struggle with her sister getting things before her. I have an older sister and Danyael has two older siblings so we both experienced being the youngest, but there is definitely a difference when you're SO close in age. Chloe's experience is different from my own or my wife's.

And I don't want to discount Julianna's experience here. She is often in a position where she feels a sense of guilt that she is just slightly more advanced or has access to different things than her younger sister. This is magnified for her particularly because of her incredibly strong sense of empathy. I think they both struggle occasionally with the totally normal kid/teenager battle between *what's good for me* versus *what's good for her*—selfish versus selfless. I think that is a normal human struggle and Julianna and Chloe are humans, so it plays a part.

The good thing, I think, with Chloe and Julianna is that their personalities are SO different. While they have lots in common, like to spend time together, get on each other's nerves, and share secrets from time to time (working together to keep secrets from Danyael and me), they do have a tendency and the confidence (mostly) to be comfortable with who they are to themselves and not try to be *like* the other. Danyael and I have always told them that they are going to be close—in age literally and as sisters/friends hopefully—for their whole lives.

We encourage them to lean into their differences. It is what makes them who they are. We didn't and don't have any real control over their nature but certainly did and do over the nurture part.

CHAPTER TEN

Poopy Potty—Age 2

Poopy potty.

That's what we called the toilet. As a grown adult, I fully understand that we do more on the toilet than just make poopy. We visit the poopy potty multiple times a day. Some of us like to sit on the poopy potty for 45 minutes at a time. For both Julianna and Chloe, we followed a similar routine. Once they each got to the stage where they were no longer pleased to be sitting in a dirty diaper, we knew it was time.

Accuracy . . . that is what we dealt with for a while. Julianna would tell us quite a bit that she wanted to go sit on the poopy potty, but 49 out of 50 times, it was a false alarm. I didn't think she had figured out the difference between a cramp perhaps, or a minor urge, and the immediate need to sit and relieve.

That being said, we don't want to miss the opportunity. What if this is the one out of 50 times and she actually drops that deuce? We figured—optimistically—that it would only take one successful deposit and we'd be all set. There was a time, a few months before we really started to practice, that she actually managed to successfully use the toilet. It was probably right before bath time and we probably just put her on the toilet, naked, to wait while we got the water ready.

It turns out she wasn't really ready.

Part of me (a good part) thought she was using the potty as an excuse to stall. She always seemed to want to sit on the poopy potty right before bed and definitely not until after we had gotten her into pajamas and about to get into the crib. But what do you do? What if the deposit was actually ready to arrive? We didn't want to miss it. . . .

There were times, like one day when we spent a good chunk of the afternoon at my sister's house, a safe place to practice doing just that. Julianna was regularly asking to go to the potty. We obliged, a few times. One of those times, I just put her on the toilet, with the lid down and her pants on. That satisfied her. So, we continued the journey . . . until we got home that very same day. I suppose we could try one more time. Picture it, she was sitting on the poopy potty. I was sitting in front of her with a book . . . and then . . . she froze. I remember the look in her eyes. The world froze with her. Was it really going to happen?

Activity in the bowl!

In retrospect, the following played out in an oddly similar way to when both of my girls were born: She was clutching the side of the potty seat and barely breathing. I instructed her in as positive a voice as I could muster that it was—and always will be—a good idea to breathe. I followed up by demonstrating.

Do it with me. You know you want to.

Breathe in . . .

Breathe out . . .

Breathe in . . .

Breathe out . . .

She actually did the breathing exercise with me. The breathing sounds were the only sounds she was making. She had stopped talking so she could fully concentrate. Her eyes were locked on to mine. Her knuckles were white from gripping the side of the potty seat as tight as those newborn-sized diapers two weeks after she was born. She was in the zone—focused on the matter at hand. What happened next is a moment I'll never forget and I'll never be able to fully explain. She was clearly not finished yet and still not making any noise, she threw both her hands straight up into the air like an NFL referee as if to signal, TOUCHDOWN!

I imagine she was experiencing a combination of joy, pride, victory, and relief, all at once. She finished up, still doing her breathing exercise, snapped out of her trance, and immediately wanted to get off the poopy potty and see her work. This is, of course, a rite of passage and something that I believe she still might do. Who could blame her—or anyone? You must appreciate your work.

"Daddy, can I pick out my own underwear?"

Not quite but I love the confidence.

Chloe had a pretty similar path but a different backstory. Chloe had all sorts of digestion and constipation issues when she was a baby. This made the pooping experience a pretty big . . . well . . . pain in the ass. Pooping was never a fun time for her. From very early on, Chloe was taking MiraLAX, and we would roll her knees around her stomach and try to help her move things along. For a good amount of time when she was a baby/toddler, we had to resort to using a suppository to help her out. That experience was fun for exactly nobody but did give her quite a bit of relief. Five minutes after I'd set her up with one of those, it would be like Mount Vesuvius erupting. She would always feel so incredibly great after those times that I think it actually helped to block out how miserable the experience was leading up to it.

Once she got old enough to sit on the toilet, we started doing that—earlier than we did with Julianna. This was because we figured this would be easier for her: Gravity and the Bowl. While we were confident that everything would work out and she'd figure out how to use the toilet like her sister, you just never know when it's going to click.

So here she is, sitting on the toilet. It was right before we were going to give her a bath, so she was naked. Now, my daughters—Chloe in particular—have always been quite inquisitive, about everything. This whole process was fascinating for her. I'm sitting with her and she bends over because she tells me she thinks she feels something happening!

Oh, how exciting this was.

She told me she wants to watch. Outstanding. It's like a poopper-view.

She bends over so she can get a good view (how I long for the days of being that flexible). She is just staring at her nether region waiting and waiting. Nothing is happening, but she is stubborn and persistent. I told her we can wait for as long as it takes. This was thrilling!

She then sits up and says it's not happening.

Please remember that she was naked and bent over to watch her own machinery work from the front.

Before I can react, she says the following, and I truly wish I was making this up: "Daddy, do I have a tongue in my vagina?"

I'm going to let you think about that for a moment. Yeah, I think I'm okay if we just move on. Yes. I'm good with going to the next chapter now.

CHAPTER ELEVEN

Reading; Their Minds—Ages 2–5

I don't remember how old I was when people stopped reading to me at my bedtime.

Those days, I got read to most nights. At some point, the girls' bedtime went from us reading to them, to them reading to us. I find the whole thing fascinating. Both girls always enjoyed books. We went through all the same phases you went through:

- **Phase 1:** Board books with six pages and giant colorful shapes and things.
- **Phase 2:** Board books with 12 pages, two words on a page, and most of the corners of said pages worn down by drool.
- **Phase 3:** Board books with 27 pages of rhyming *poetry* that we can read each night—sometimes twice—for six months straight. This time, the corners have bite marks on them and many of the pages are peeling off of their boards from the drool.

- **Phase 4:** Paper books that are square-shaped with stories about our favorite characters. Many of these pages have rips near the binding because, you know, everyone wants to help turn the pages and turning from the inside half of the page always results in a paper rip.
- **Phase 5:** Gigantic hardcover books with pages that fold out and pieces that move and inevitably get ripped out that you later read anyway and just pretend are still there even though Elmo's body is missing his oscillating head.
- **Phase 6:** Dr. Seuss books that will hopefully not be *One fish, two fish, red fish, blue fish* because—and I'm not kidding—it is like 350 pages long.
- **Phase 7:** *One fish, two fish, red fish, blue fish* for the eighth night in a row where you only read the left pages and don't get caught.
- **Phase 8:** *One fish, two fish, red fish, blue fish* for the eighth night in a row where you try and only read the left pages but DO get caught.

This is the turning point . . .

Wait, did my daughter just recognize that I skipped pages and parts of the story were missing?

And so it goes.

More complicated books with more words leads to pointing my finger at each word as I go so we can all follow along. At least now, in my head, I am helping to teach the girls how to read.

- **Phase 9:** We read Shel Silverstein's *The Giving Tree* and harken back to our youth and how wonderful (but sort of sad) a story it is.

In fact, I love *The Giving Tree* so much, I go for more Shel Silverstein books and realize that I haven't heard any of his work since

I was a kid and maybe I never really paid much attention. I attain this understanding now, as an adult, because I started to read a few of the short poems and come across one like this:

> *So what if nobody came?*
> *I'll have all the ice cream and tea,*
> *And I'll laugh with myself,*
> *And I'll dance with myself,*
> *And I'll sing, "Happy Birthday to me!"*

That's "Happy Birthday" by Shel Silverstein.

Here we have a story that comes with a beautiful illustration of a kid with lit candles buried in his head and hair that seems to be melting down his face laughing to himself about how much fun it will be when nobody shows up to his birthday party.

Sweet dreams, kids.

That's when you realize that maybe we should take a break from Shel, but hey, reading is fun and definitely not depressing.

- **Phase 10:** We break out some old board books and practice reading again! You read this page and I'll read the next page.
- **Phase 11:** You read two pages to me and I'll read two pages to you.
- **Phase 12:** You suddenly realize that you can no longer spell words to your spouse when your kid asks "Daddy, where are you going to take that shit?"

By this phase, Julianna and Chloe are both starting to really read. You realize that there's a very real possibility that one of these days, probably sooner rather than later, your kids will discover and really understand that you had been writing a blog documenting their childhood and that they will want to read it and then roll their eyes at you—or worse.

- **Phase 13:** We sit in bed and I listen as the entire book is read to me. I'm told that we'll *read and show*. This means that she reads the page and then turns the book around to show me the pictures like in school. This is cute, but takes about 10 times longer to get through the book than if I were reading, and honestly, the plots (and I use that word loosely) in these books are not particularly compelling for me and totally predictable.

- **Phase 14:** Now I sit and they read the entire book and just want me to be present. They don't need to show the pictures; they just want the company. Every now and then I get to read to them and it's a pleasure. Mostly I'm just sitting, staring at the ceiling, and hoping not to fall asleep, or hoping I do fall asleep. I can't decide.

Each night at this phase, I would ask, "Are you reading to me, or am I reading to you?"

One of the nights that Chloe wanted to read to me, she picked out her book and brought it over to bed. Sometimes it was a chapter book and sometimes it was one that has pictures. This particular time it was the latter.

I found myself staring at her, in a sort of awe, truly enjoying watching her enjoy reading. She turned each page and then took a few moments to look at the pictures. She took her time, really soaking in what's happening before she started to read and get into it. In the off chance that she ran into a word she couldn't pronounce, she pointed at it and waited, knowing/hoping that I was still paying enough attention and would help. These help requests progressively become fewer and farther between.

I love reading and while I have always been confident that my kids would enjoy it as well, it was so much fun to see it playing out. I always loved going in their bedrooms at night to check on them and then finding a book on their bed with a bookmark in it that they were reading after bedtime but before they were ready to fall asleep. It's one thing when they are *performing* for me and another when they are doing it for their own enjoyment.

I loved watching them figure it all out while realizing that there are endless stories to enjoy. This is why I was and have always been a sucker for the bookstore. Any time we were near a bookstore we would go in and I'd let them pick out books. There were even times when I was fairly certain they wouldn't actually read *that one*, but the risk was worth it. Just to see them get excited about whatever adventure was happening between the front and back covers was thrilling for me. So what if they were a little spoiled. There are worse things to be spoiled about.

I will say, though, that after spending a lot of time reading with both of them for many years and really paying attention to the content, like Shel Silverstein (whom I always loved as a kid), I realized that many, if not most, stories involved harrowing plot points and somewhat scary—or at least creepy—details. There were plenty of times when I felt like we were about to have to have a discussion about why that boy was celebrating his birthday alone (maybe it was that he had candles growing out of his head and was shunned by his classmates). Sometimes there would be conversations and sometimes—if I got lucky—we'd cruise right on by, because the illustrations were so compelling or the rhythm of the story was so interesting.

Each time I would read a new one of these books that had a more *negative* feel to it, even though they almost all inevitably ended happily, I got to thinking that it would be great if there were more that were just purely positive; that there were more stories that had no conflict. I'm not suggesting that conflict is bad or that there aren't strong lessons that a child can learn from understanding a conflict and its resolution. I'm just saying that sometimes it might be nice if we just had fun stories that made you smile and you didn't have to worry about any of it along the way (speaking as a parent of kids who both got anxious about the sad parts of stories).

So . . . I wrote one. . . .

Interlude

Goody Blueshoes

I once heard a story about Goody Blueshoes.
Goody is a girl with some interesting views.
You probably won't hear of her on the news.
It is a story you can share, if you so choose.

She was an everyday girl who liked doing good.
She liked being good as any girl could.
She could be as good as any girl should.
She should be as good as any girl would.

She has lots of friends and plays a whole lot.
Because playing and friending was fun, she thought.
She always uses nice words and shares all her toys.
She plays with all people, both the girls and the boys.

She always says please and follows with thank you.
She never tells a fib and only speaks what is true.
She likes to eat fruits and vegetables too.
She leaves her mouth closed when she's going to chew.

She tries not to fuss or whine or complain.
She exercises her body as well as her brain.
She loves to read books and play in the rain.
I suspect when she drives she'll stay in her lane.

She lets others go first and holds open the doors.
She makes her own bed and does all of her chores.
She stays with her parents when she visits the stores.
She puts sunscreen and bug spray on when she goes
    outdoors.

She's a pretty good kid and tries to stay humble.
She learns from mistakes when she has a stumble.

She'll never be perfect but does the best she can do.
She's a good girl now and will be a good woman too.

Goody is good and has shoes that are blue.
But shoes don't really matter, so she may as well be you.

PART III

Development

CHAPTER TWELVE

The Santa Clause—Age 3

I love Santa.

Well, I love what Santa represents for so many people around the world—*magic.*

Santa represents something magical and whimsical—something innocent, hopeful, and happy. Who couldn't use more of all of those things?

One of the greatest joys of being a parent for me has been to see the wonder of discovery through my daughters' eyes—the innocence of youth. We all share a pretty complicated world and part of what makes it so complicated is the effort many of us parents make to protect that very complexity from our children, for as long as possible. And why not?

They have plenty of time to worry about worrying about things but when they were toddlers, I always imagined this protective semi-permeable bubble around them that only allowed in information and environmental factors that passed our censors. We know this bubble doesn't last forever and isn't perfect, but for as long as it can help protect them, why not lean in?

I never believed in Santa growing up. My family didn't, and doesn't, celebrate Christmas. I remember my friends who did, however, and I also remember not *spoiling* it for them. I don't remember why I wouldn't have. I don't think anyone told me not to say anything. Let's be honest, the Santa concept is pretty far-fetched. It's almost as ridiculous as a magical bunny that hides eggs in your backyard. For starters—and I'm no biologist or zoo-keeper—but bunnies do not lay eggs, so I'm not sure where this whole myth came from but even still, I'm into it and I'm into Santa.

Bruce Willis's character is dead the entire movie. (#spoileralert)

We, the people, generally love spoiling things but for some reason, there's always been some universal and unspoken rule about Santa. Many people really love letting other people know when they know something that they think you don't know. Knowledge is power. So why then, is this secret one that we all collectively keep? Deep down, I believe we all want to believe in magic and that is what Santa represents.

When the girls were both at or close to the point where other kids they saw at school might start talking about Santa, we had a decision to make. We knew that it was inevitable that they would come home from preschool and tell us about how their friends were all talking about the toys that Santa brought them and ask why Santa didn't bring them anything. Well, let's see:

1. *"Santa didn't come here because he only brings toys to the nice kids."*—No.
2. *"Santa didn't come here because we don't have a tree in our living room."*—No.
3. *"Santa must have forgotten you."*—No.
4. *"Santa just comes to Jewish houses after he's finished with all the other houses."* [run to toy store]—No.
5. *"Santa doesn't exist."*—Probably not.

I'd hate it if my kids ruined the dream for the other kids since the spirit of Christmas and a child's wonder are really fun to watch. You see the kids in the mall get so excited to sit on Santa's lap, forcing themselves to look right past any amount of rational logic that suggests that THE Santa happens to be in your local mall all afternoon. You might not have been one, but we all know kids who go to sleep on Christmas Eve all excited to find out what Santa will have left for them under their trees the next morning. To this day, I still love Christmas Eve and all the *potential energy* and excitement in the air that comes from thinking about all those kids who celebrate Christmas going to sleep early (I assume—because I would have) so they can get out of Santa's way and, let's be honest, the sooner you go to sleep the sooner you wake up on Christmas morning.

Here's the thing: people who celebrate Christmas have more built-in magic opportunities in things like Santa and the Easter Bunny than many others. People who are Jewish, like my family, don't. The oil lasting for eight nights instead of one doesn't provide the same kind of impact. Hanukkah is fun and all, but not an incredibly important Jewish holiday; certainly not as important religiously as Christmas is for Christians. Here's what I'll do for you. I'll even throw in our next most exciting holiday that has a *magical* feel to it—Passover.

Surprisingly enough, while Moses parting the Red Sea is pretty impressive but unfortunately (or fortunately depending on your perspective) comes just after the Egyptian water is turned into blood, a swarm of frogs hops up into your streets, lice for everyone, a fly infestation (and I'm not talking about the kind that you get when your kids leave a bowl of fruit on the counter overnight), all of the livestock being killed (McDonald's be damned), a breakout of boils (sounds sexy), terrible hail storms (New England Jews laugh this one off), swarms of locusts (because the flies were not vile enough), total darkness for three days (no generators back then), and then the crème de la creme: slaying of first born Egyptian children (that'll show 'em).

You can have all that *joy* that we Jewish people celebrate . . . or a chubby guy in a red suit visiting children on one night, by jamming his ass down your chimney, eating your cookies, and leaving toys under a tree in your living room.

While I'm sure, like me, you have pretty mixed emotions about the choice and it is quite enticing, I'm not sure this is really an apples-to-apples type of comparison.

My kids don't get to believe in magic for very long in life, relatively speaking, but for as long as they can, I'm in on the Christmas story and I don't regret it at all.

We did end up telling the kids about Santa—he only visits the children who celebrate Christmas—but that doesn't mean you don't also get toys. We tell them that one of the differences is that we get to celebrate for eight days. That's right; Hanukkah lasts eight times longer than Christmas despite those of you who don't care about the Earth and put in their best effort to use all the electricity to trick me into thinking it lasts longer by leaving your lights up on your house through February. Oh yeah, there's no naughty/nice situation with Hanukkah. Just do what my grandmother did each year: give me the Toys "R" Us pull-out from the newspaper and a crayon and I'll circle what I want. Do what my Aunt Marcia did and just take me to Toys "R" Us and let me spend a few hours roaming the aisles—looking at every toy (front and back)—and picking out what I want. Suck on that Christmas.

. . . Oh, bonus: my kids don't even need to share their cookies. Ho ho humbug.

But I will tell you about another piece of *magic* I cared very deeply about as a parent. But first, I just wanted to write a sentence or two about my Bar Mitzvah when I was 13 years old because maybe it explains my obsession with the current topic.

I'm sure you are wondering about the theme of my Bar Mitzvah: Magic. No, not *The Gathering* type. We're talking David Copperfield stuff. I've always enjoyed magic. I took magic classes as a kid and to this day, I use little sleight-of-hand tricks to very successfully impress people. Trust me, it's a hit.

Anyhow . . . here's a piece of magic I was very supportive of with my kids that has nothing to do with religion: the Tooth Fairy. When Julianna lost her first tooth, she received a letter from the Tooth Fairy. It went like this (her note was handwritten—so you'll forgive the font here):

To my dearest Julianna,

Losing a tooth can be so much fun,
And losing your first is the very best one.
As your teeth fall out, I can come and collect them,
I will take care of each and every one like a precious gem.
I'm ever so quiet and come very late,
I'll be careful to not wake you because sleep is so great,
Of course, brushing your teeth is more important than ever,
But you already knew that because you seem to be so clever.
As your baby teeth fall out and your big teeth obey gravity,
Keep brushing and flossing so you don't get a cavity.
Take care of your sister Chloe who I know you love dearly.
Congratulations and I'm very proud of you . . .

Love,

The Tooth Fairy

I know what you're thinking: you weren't aware that the Tooth Fairy wrote letters to kids. Lean in for a second so I can tell you a secret: She didn't write it. I did.

I came up with this wacky idea to write a letter. I even went as far as asking a coworker, who had much better penmanship than I have, to write it out. I decided it couldn't sound at all like my voice and couldn't look like my writing. This whole thing went over like winning Powerball. It was a massive success. Julianna was thrilled to receive a personal letter.

Unfortunately, I made a terrible mistake because what I actually did—without thinking it through enough—was commit to 19 more letters for Julianna and 20 for Chloe. All I had to do was have the Tooth Fairy say something like:

> Don't be greedy and expect more of these letters from me.
> I'm the Tooth Fairy and I didn't grow on a tree.
> There are lots of children and lots of teeth under the sun.
> You only get a personal letter from me for the first one.

But I didn't do that. Do you even know how many children there are in the world losing teeth every day? Santa gets a ton of attention for one night of work each year. The Tooth Fairy does it 3-6-5. She puts in the work.

Because we are Jewish, the girls don't get to experience a lot of magic like their Christian friends. They don't get to experience Santa or the Easter Bunny. I wanted to make sure that they get to believe in the Tooth Fairy and get to have as great an experience as possible. I love that they both bought in and I hoped—a bit skeptically—that it lasted for a long time. There were definitely times when I thought they guessed it might be me.

That's just absurd.

But then there are times, when I thought for all the bravado of thinking they figured it out, something happened where I'd be convinced that they still believed.

You see, the girls decided that they would write letters to the Tooth Fairy when their teeth fell out and there was one letter in particular that I remember sneaking a peek at which got me a little emotional.

Julianna wrote, among other things, that she wasn't sure exactly how many teeth she had lost, but thought she was close to losing all of her baby teeth (she was right). She wrote that once they were all out, she was going to miss the visits from the Tooth Fairy; that she was *bummed*.

And that is the magic.

Julianna went to sleep that night, her letter sitting with her tooth (on her bookshelf—because who wants a stranger, even a magical one, creeping around your pillow while you sleep), exhausted from what happened to also be her first day at a new school (middle school), exhausted from not having her stuff or her bedroom for the past two months (she had been at summer camp), exhausted from a long summer of fun and craziness . . .

And still believing in magic.

CHAPTER THIRTEEN

Anger Management: All Ages

I'm a pretty even-keeled, mild-mannered type of person. It takes quite a lot to get me going. In fact, I can count on one hand how many times I've really lost my temper in my life, and when I think back to those times, it gives me the feeling inside like the feeling you get when someone runs their fingernails down a chalkboard. The last time I remember losing my temper was long before my kids were born.

My point is, it used to be hard to push my buttons enough to really bother me. Don't get me wrong, a lot of things annoy or anger me, many of which most people would probably be annoyed to find out annoy me. My poor wife has to suffer through them on a regular basis so I'm certainly not the poster child for perfection.

So far, and lucky for me, the only people who have managed to push my buttons on any sort of consistent pattern are my kids, and I've been trying to figure out why that is.

To be clear—it is all relative. Danyael and I have talked about this from time to time: We believe we have fantastic, wonderful, and brilliant kids. I know lots of people say that about their kids but when I say it, it is definitely true (unlike when you say it).

It's just that sometimes . . . ugggg . . . you know, right?

On the way home from school one day, Julianna said she couldn't wait to get home so she could go help Mommy cook dinner. She had started doing this for pretty much each meal and we were encouraging it in whichever safe ways were possible. She was also clearing her own plate and helping clean up (sometimes). She literally insisted on washing her own hands after a meal and, I mean, she was not even three years old yet when this started happening.

But when she would rip a toy out of Chloe's hand or she refused to let us take the Band-Aid off her neck (which she had on because once her neck was stiff the idea was hatched that Band-Aids work for stiff muscles—and that worked—but now has turned into an occasional crutch even without a stiff neck). We should have owned stock in Band-Aid based on the amount of product we were using.

At that same time, Chloe wasn't even two years old. When we would get to school, she always thanked me for driving. When we got to our street coming home from anywhere, she would thank me for driving. When I would sneeze, she would say, "Bless you Daddy." She always used her pleases and thank yous, and she would literally eat any kind of food without complaint.

But when it was time to go out in the New England winter and she would vehemently refuse to wear a hat, well, that wasn't great. Or how she insisted on not wearing socks at home—ever—which meant we had to throw one sock on her foot and then distract her until we can get the foot-matching shoe on to lock it in place followed by finding the other sock that might have gotten tossed somewhere and then the other shoe.

So how is it that those little few and far between moments caused such emotional/mental distress for me?

There aren't many people in my life whom I let get close enough that I have to, or can, drop my guard. So close in fact, that when they kick me in the balls, figuratively speaking (and literally from time to time), it hurts a lot more.

Here's the cringey thing: I wouldn't trade it for anything. I love almost every second of it, and in retrospect, probably every second. The good times outweigh the annoying, button-pushing moments by so much that they probably aren't even worth mentioning. I just find the exploration of how my kids, of all people, are the ones who do the best job of occasionally getting under my skin to be interesting.

So what if she didn't want to wear a hat? Well . . . it is cold out.

What if she didn't want to let me wash her face? Lots of kids walk around with their hair plastered to their upper lip via snot cement.

I don't know. Maybe I had unrealistic expectations, but shouldn't someone who thinks The Backyardigans are classic rock be a little more reasonable? I mean, when this started, they were a combined age of almost 5.

The good news, you ask? It definitely has not gotten better. In 2024, they are both in high school and they still don't wear jackets in the winter. This time it's because they can't be bothered (like any of the students) to use their assigned lockers and carrying a jacket around all day is like . . . you know?

That towel Chloe used after she took her shower? That's good for at least another few showers, right? After all, you are drying off your clean body with it. Nope. Her laundry hamper is overflowing with towels. We must use a new one for each shower. In some cases, we must use multiple towels for a shower because our hair requires different toweling than our bodies.

Maybe it's this: the people who are most likely to really be able to push my buttons are the ones who are close enough to me to reach them because I would never distance myself from them.

These are the people I want to have in my life forever. When other people annoy me, I can just create distance between myself and them. It's probably why I have a large group of friends and a small group of great friends.

If you annoy me at work well, I can just close my office door or go home. If you annoy me at the grocery store with your 19 items in the 15 or fewer checkout line, I can give you a satisfyingly dirty look behind your back. If you park your car straddling two spaces because for some reason you/your car has some sort of entitlement issue, I can put a kindergarten-style *Way-to-Go* postcard on your windshield. But if you're one of my daughters? I'll just huff and puff and then have to get over it.

They're stuck with me.

CHAPTER FOURTEEN

A Star is Born—Ages 3–5

Julianna participated in a weekly ballet class when she was a toddler. We also tried gymnastics, which garnered mixed results. We had high hopes for ballet. My wife and I would alternate who took her to class. The parents would all sit outside while the girls in the class *danced*. The goal is to get the class on stage for a routine at the dance school's annual recital.

Classes and rehearsals would run from September through May, once a week, to put together this routine. The final routine lasts just short of 45 total seconds.

The recital happened and it very well may have been the best 45 seconds of my parenting life (that's what she said).

After that first time, I imagined I was witnessing the first of what will likely be millions of performances my kids are part of. It was the first time either of them stood on stage, without either of their parents with them, in a costume, in front of an auditorium filled with parents, behind a curtain, in the dark, waiting for the curtain to open and the music to start.

Two weeks prior to the curtain going up, during class in the studio, she put her costume on for the first time. All the parents were in there and we were going to do a run-through. One note in, Julianna decided that she did not want to dance in front of everyone.

This didn't bode well for the recital. This is a girl who would demand that we sit on the couch in the living room while she stood on the *stage* and played a kid's guitar and sang songs to us. She would tell me that when she grows up, she wants to be a diva. Just kidding. She actually told us she wants to be a *doctor for babies*, but time will tell whether or not that holds up (it mostly hasn't). Needless to say, given her performative personality, we figured she'd love being able to stand up on a real stage and perform for a large group of people.

A few days before the recital, she had a dress rehearsal on the actual stage. There was not a huge audience, but she got up there on stage, hands covering her ears to protect her from the . . . volume, waving at Mommy with her elbow. Then the music started and she went right into action. She didn't miss a beat. We were hopeful. We shall see. . . .

The day of the recital arrives; nerves start to kick in when we see how many people are in the lobby waiting to get in. And you should have seen Julianna. She seemed pretty calm. Her class would be up first, so I didn't need too much oxygen or a Xanax. We followed the extremely strict procedures put in place by some dance moms who, let's just say, were probably taking this a bit too seriously and treating this like their own personal *Dancing with the Stars* audition. We dropped Julianna off backstage to hang out with her class while we went and found seats.

Eventually, after what felt like hours, the lights dimmed a bit. We saw little feet scurrying under the curtain's bottom edge. Still hopeful. . . . The lights went out and the curtain started to open. The next part was a bit of a blur.

I think they started pumping onion through the ventilation system. I'm not sure what was going on and to this day I can't be certain of the cause, but I had a slightly difficult time seeing clearly. The lights came up, she immediately waved to some strangers she assumed was us but weren't because they were sitting in the same place we had been for the rehearsal, and then the music started. . . .

And she did not miss a beat.

Ear-to-ear grin the whole time (both on her face and ours).

She did the whole routine, all 45 seconds of it, with the grace and elegance of . . . well . . . of a three-year-old girl who can't wait to get a grilled cheese after she's finished. It was perfect. She loved it. We loved it. She loved getting flowers after. She loved her grilled cheese. She loved her costume (and didn't want to take if off for hours). She loved being on the stage.

A star was born.

I'm doomed.

Cut to September 2011—just four months later. Weekly ballet class began again. Same teacher as last year. Different classroom. Different group of girls. Different song (this year the song is "Here Comes the Sun" by The Beatles. Same routine (essentially):

> *Here comes the sun, [doo doo doo doo]*
> *{Hands to the left}*

This year she had three things working in her favor:

- She's already done the routine on stage in front of an auditorium filled with what must be thousands of people (not good at estimation)
- She has three friends from her school in the class with her
- She is four months older

> *Here comes the sun, [doo doo doo doo]*
> *{Hands to the right}*

Classes were fun. She became an old pro. Nothing fazes her except occasionally (regularly) having to leave class in the middle for a potty break (didn't have to deal with that last year).

Oh no . . . what if she has a pee-pee accident during the show in May?

> *It's all right . . .*
> *{Hands over head and do the spin thing}*

The months go on. Rehearsals are oddly similar to last year. They say repetition, repetition, repetition. They don't say repetition, repetition, repetition, repetition, repetition, repetition, repetition, repetition, repetition, repetition, repetition, repetition, repetition, repetition, repetition—but it certainly feels that way to me after what was literally nine months of this routine followed by four months off followed by nine more months of the same routine to a different song.

> *Little darling, it's been a long, cold, lonely winter.*
> *Little darling, it feels like years since it's been here.*
> *{Toe point thing and letter 'P' leg move x 2}*

See? Ain't that the truth. Meanwhile, she's having the time of her life. If I remember correctly, there was a significant part of last year's cycle when we'd have to be in the room with her during class. Times when she didn't want to go in at all. Now she was putting her ballet shoes on and running into class on her own.

> *Here comes the sun, [doo doo doo doo]*
> *Here comes the sun, and I say*
> *It's all right . . .*
> *{Hands to the left}*

You know, maybe she was having a great time and it just didn't matter that it was exactly the same thing as last year.

> *Little darling, the smiles returning to the faces.*
> *Little darling, it seems like years since it's been here.*

Here comes the sun.
Here comes the sun, and I say
It's all right . . .
{Hands to the right}

Spring rolls around. The new outrageously expensive costume
(similar to the one we justified last year because we could use it
as a play costume after, but never did) gets ordered again. The
StubHub-priced ticket purchases happen—to get the collection
of relatives, cousins, and Broadway scouts in for the recital. You'd
be shocked at the aftermarket prices for these types of recitals.

The seats in the same auditorium were found.

The curtain in the same auditorium was closed.

The lights in the same auditorium went out.

The curtain in the same auditorium opened.

Sun, sun, sun, here it comes.
Sun, sun, sun, here it comes.
Sun, sun, sun, here it comes.
Sun, sun, sun, here it comes.
Sun, sun, sun, here it comes.
{Big giant circle with everyone holding hands and chassé
moves}—(Yup, I Googled the spelling.)

The crowd starts applauding wildly for the circle move (I clap
too, but I'm not nearly as impressed as these other suckers in the
audience). The girls are all smiling ear to ear again. But whether
or not they would be able to get back to their spots and finish the
dance remains to be seen . . .

Little darling, I feel that ice is slowly melting.
Little darling, it seems like years since it's been clear.
Here comes the sun, [doo doo doo doo]
Here comes the sun, and I say
It's all right.
{Back to spots for a final hands to the left and right}

I didn't know what the next year's routine would bring (but I had a sneaking suspicion) and I suppose it didn't really matter. It was awesome again. She had fun. She got on stage again, this time with zero apprehension or maybe even better: apprehension that she just dealt with on her own. She smiled. She didn't cover her ears. She did the routine. She didn't have a pee-pee accident (I wish I could make the same claim for myself).

> *Here comes the sun*
> *Here comes the sun, and I say*
> *It's all right.*
> *It's all right.*
> *{Walk off stage to thunderous applause}*

It is. It is ALL right.

CHAPTER FIFTEEN

My Oversensitivity, Not Theirs—Ages 4–5

Julianna spent a good amount of time in the *questioning everything* phase. Chloe was never *not* in that phase.

Why? Because Julianna wanted to know how everything worked and the reasons things happened. Chloe also wanted to know that, so she could decide if she would participate.

Why? Because Julianna is generally inquisitive and ultimately relentless, but Chloe, well, she's testing you. I suspect that most, if not all, kids go through this phase for at least some amount of time.

Because.

Before we did anything, or before someone visited us, we liked to tell the girls about whatever or whomever it was. This seemed to minimize the stress on the new activity, person, place, or thing. Neither Julianna nor Chloe were great with *just going with the flow* when they were younger (although Julianna was always better at it). Now, Julianna is very laid back and willing to go with that flow, but Chloe, well, she's still not satisfied with not knowing what to expect. So, about that one time when a friend and former coworker of mine was coming over to visit . . . I was telling Julianna about him when she asked the following question:

"Is he white or brown?"

Well, that was a new one for which I was not prepared. A bunch of things went through my head at that moment including, but not limited to:

+ Should I be embarrassed?
+ What if she made a comment like that in public?
+ Did she say things like that in school?
+ Was it a big deal at all?
+ Was I being too sensitive?
+ Was she not being sensitive enough?

And then I decided that it was actually more of an issue for me than her. She was asking in a purely observational and expectation-setting way. She was just wondering and rightfully didn't have any reason to think there would be anything wrong with that question. Maybe it is me who is being too sensitive. Maybe.

In her fictional adventures of that time, "Yo Gabba Gabba," "Mickey Mouse Clubhouse," "Sesame Street," etc., she learned that there were all sorts of different-looking people. The differences weren't explicitly talked about—they just were different. I think it was a lesson these shows tried to subtly and constantly teach as part of their inherent DNA, not as a specific topic. Aside from the fact that in real life, she wasn't going to see a 7-foot-tall, one-eyed, red pickle-looking thing (what's up "Yo Gabba Gabba's" Muno?) on the streets (if so, run), it's great. I think "Sesame Street" always has done a nice job with these sorts of lessons and all the other shows do it, too.

Around that time (and always if you're me or Danyael), we had been listening to a lot of music from the Broadway musical "Wicked." Julianna wanted to know about the characters who were singing and wanted to see pictures of them. She noticed that Elphaba was green (for those who don't know/care, Elphaba was the character who turned into the *wicked* witch). She asked, "Why is she green?" Just wondering. Just another example of someone who looks different. I told her it was because she just got off a whale watch on Cape Cod that involved three hours of boating out into choppy seas to see humpback whales for 18 minutes before three more hours of boating back to shore, all while enjoying cups of coffee that only cost $0.05 each. Shout-out to The Bubster (one of my grandmothers).

I didn't actually tell her the whale watch bit. That was an actual thing that happened to my grandmother and mother when we went on a whale watch when I was a kid.

Anyhow, I don't know if I responded the right way but here's what I said about the friend who was visiting: "His skin color is white. He's very nice and you'll like playing with him. Who do you know whose skin color is brown?" (I wanted to get a sense of what she was differentiating or how she was making the connection). She listed a few people and we talked about how much we liked them too. Then I asked her if she knew anyone who has green skin. She of course mentioned Elphaba. We talked about red skin (Muno—"Yo Gabba Gabba") and pink polka-dotted skin (Uniqua—"Backyardigans"). And that was it. No big deal. From there, it was on to what we were going to have for breakfast.

One of the most important things for me was to raise kids who are accepting of everyone, no matter anything. It is something I was/am always sensitive about.

I want her to know it is okay to observe differences. She was different. I was different. We all were. Fine.

I now think it was cool that she asked because she was wondering, not because she cared one way or the other. Because she was in a stage where she was starting to figure out there was a world all around her. I started to realize that I could, but shouldn't, be afraid of that exploration and I shouldn't, but could, be over sensitive to it or she might start thinking there's something wrong with differences.

White, Black, Red Sox, Yankees, Gay, Straight, Grouch, Ballerina, Jewish, Muslim, Democrat, Republican. It shouldn't matter to us. It never mattered to her or Chloe.

Why?

Just because.

CHAPTER SIXTEEN

The Great Pyramids—Age 4

"Daddy, where does the pyramid come from?"

I got those types of questions regularly. My mother was once asked by Chloe why she couldn't see the moon during the day. What can I say, my kids are nerd-wannabes like their daddy. It makes me very proud.

"Daddy, where does the pyramid come from?"

Context: Julianna was sitting on the toilet right before bed one night (a lot of our best conversations happened on or near a toilet).

I said, "Julianna, what do you mean? People built them."

"No, where does the pyramid come from?"

I said, "I'm not sure what you mean." (as she looked around the room).

So, I start to look around the room trying to figure out what she was referencing.

"Daddy, where does MY pyramid come from? Does it come from here?" (pointing to her butt).

"Umm . . ." (confused).

"Does my pyramid come from here?" (pointing again).

"Wait," I said, "Do you mean, 'Where does your PERIOD come from?'"

"Yes."

"Umm. . . ."

She recently came across a tampon in our bathroom (not mine) and asked what it was. Was it something you eat? No. Was it something mommy eats? No. What did it do? Ask mommy.

She must have asked mommy. . . .

Now she wants to know where her pyramid comes from.

Egypt.

Question mark?

Exclamation point!

CHAPTER SEVENTEEN

Stuck on the Window—Age 5

You know the endless chain of questions your kid asks?

You know how at the first question you ask yourself if you should *engage* and subject yourself to the endless chain because you know what happens if you answer the first question?

You know how you inevitably do end up *engaging*—which leads to the next question?

You know how after the first few answers, you've chosen a *direction*, either based in truth or maybe not so much, but mostly optimized for how quickly you can get to the end of the thread?

You know how regardless of the level of truth, you start to corner yourself even though the questions continue?

You know how you tell yourself that *they* will run out of energy or attention for this line of questioning before you run out of answers?

You know that moment when you realize you were wrong and they are relentless no matter how many times this had already happened this week alone?

That's when I realized we were stuck on the window . . . with nowhere to go.

I like to consider myself a pretty good improviser, particularly when it comes to conversations with kids. I was a camp counselor for a long time. I enjoyed the TV show "Whose Line Is It Anyway," and frankly, I find it entertaining to challenge myself. Of course, Julianna and Chloe have at least some DNA in common with me and also seemed to enjoy the challenge, but they weren't in it for the entertainment. They were craving information and found a nerdy partner in me who was always willing to engage in conversation cul-de-sacs. They were trying to assign reason to life's quandaries. They were buying into the NBC "The More You Know" campaign. They were figuring that if they learn ALL the answers, there will be nothing left to be scared of.

One day, Julianna was off at a birthday party with my wife (we went through a few different stretches of time where we had birthday parties or bar/bat mitzvahs essentially constantly; often multiple instances in a single weekend). Chloe and I went to do some errands. Both girls enjoyed the single-kid car rides because it meant they had exclusive rights over song selections. Song selection is still an issue to this day. Chloe chose music from the Broadway show, *Wicked*, and the song "Defying Gravity" in particular.

No matter how many times they heard this music, they both wanted to hear the story over and over again. Who is who? Who did what? Which is when? Why did how? Over and over. Therefore, it shouldn't have surprised me when that ride's bait question arrived during listen number four of "Defying Gravity":

"Daddy, what does gravity mean?"

Without pause, I accepted the challenge (I'm a nerd and can't resist, particularly when they ask me questions that I think can lead to a real science or math discussion). I asked myself quickly, "How should I explain what gravity is?" Somewhere in the back of my head I knew that she was really asking about the word in the context of the song but Captain Geek had to step in and Carpe Diem.

I came up with what I thought was a pretty good explanation: "It is the thing that keeps us stuck to the ground. Without it, we'd all be floating. In space, there's no gravity and that's why every-thing floats." And then, I came up with the big finish (or so I thought): "Imagine if there was a magnet in the middle of the Earth and we all had magnets on our . . ."

"Daddy, does Elphaba float?"

And we're hooked. Please forgive the *Wicked* references/spoil-ers ahead. . . .

"Well, sort of, it is really her broom that is floating. She's just riding it."

"How does she get on?"

"You know, she just puts one leg on one side and the other leg on the other side and as the broom goes up, it carries her with it."

"But is she floating inside the Wizard's castle?"

"Yes." (This is the moment when I am trying to end the con-versation or redirect or get her to lose interest)

"Why is she in the Wizard's castle?"

So, we're not even talking about gravity anymore, which is killing my gravity-defying nerd-high.

"She's in the castle to . . . [Oh, I don't know] . . . help the flying monkeys get back to where they belong."

"Where do they belong?"

"Well, flying monkeys are really much happier when they are living in the jungles and stuff [scientific word]."

"Are there flying monkeys in the trees behind our house?"

"No, there are no flying monkeys anywhere except in Oz."

"Does the Wizard know that Elphaba is letting the monkeys out?"

"You know, I'm not sure if the Wizard knows that."

"Do you think he knows?"

"I don't know. He's the one with the [air quotes] magical powers. I can't read his mind." (This is where I started to get snippy and resentful—at myself—for letting this go on so long).

"Take a guess."

"Umm, yes. I think he knows." (This is where I know I'm completely screwed. Either answer here leads to about a million more question possibilities and I know she's smart enough to think of them all—I'll spare you.)

"So how does Elphaba get them out?"

"I imagine she opens a window."

"You imagine or really?"

"Really." (Similar to actual monkeys, I'm sort of throwing feces around now.)

"How do they get out of the window?"

"Well, they have wings so they probably just fly out."

"What if they don't fit out the window?"

"They'll fit."

"But what if they don't?"

"I did a quick Google search and have determined that they will, indeed, fit."

"Daddy. When did you do a quick Google search? You're driving."

"I did it in my head."

"You have Google in your head?"

"Yes. No."

"Which is it?"

"What were you saying about those flying monkeys?"

"Do they take turns going out the window?"

"Yes, they have to take turns because they can't all fit at once." (Big mistake.)

"How many can fit at once?"

"So, we're stuck on the window?"

"Yes."

INTERLUDE

Today is the Day

We've established I'm a nerd with an active imagination. For as long as I can remember, my writing style has always been less of a planned type of thing and more of an *I-have-an-idea* sort of thing. In many cases, I'll have an idea for something and work on it in my head before I start typing. The following is a poem I came up with in that way. I wrote this back in December of 2013 while feeling what my daughters would refer to as *cringey*, likely while sitting on the toilet:

> I wake up each morning and just have to say,
> Yesterday was something but Today is THE day.
> With the vigor of sunrise and the flowers of May,
> Today is the day I continue on my way.
>
> Today is the day I will do something smart.
> I will draw it or paint it or create some fine art.
> I will type it or sculpt it or play it by heart.
> Whatever it is, I'm sure to take part.

Today is the day I will do something right.
I'll hold open doors and I will be polite.
I'll be cheesy and corny and won't even care.
I'll run and jump and breathe the fresh air.

Today is the day I'll be thankful for you.
For being a good person and wearing a blue shoe.
The people around me, whether many or few,
I'm lucky to have them as part of my crew.

Today is the day to make some mistakes,
To get some things wrong, because those are the breaks.
I'll learn from my faults because that's what it takes,
To get a bit better by having some aches.

Today is the day to plan for tomorrow.
When I'll take a big trip and I'll climb Kilimanjaro.
I'll move ahead and do so without sorrow,
Because today's learnings will be ready in the future
    to borrow.

Yesterday's tomorrow is where I am at,
And tomorrow's yesterday is really just that.
I'll get out and do something and be a success.
Because *defining* tomorrow is only a guess.

Today is the day to clean off the slate.
Today is the day with the most important date.
Today is the day to pull your own weight.
Today is the day to do something great.

PART IV

Growth

CHAPTER EIGHTEEN

Kindergarten—Ages 5–6

Kindergarten transition was not a smooth one for me. In May of 2013, during the run-up to kindergarten, there were a variety of orientation types of activities setup to prepare both the parents and their kids for the milestone.

That orientation was likely pretty trying for many, if not all, of the kids and for many, if not all, of the parents. Danyael and I attended a meeting at the elementary school that our daughters would attend. The meeting was with the principal and a group of oddly nervous and fidgety parents. I think it was safe to assume that at least most of us had gone through this before ourselves—as kids—so I wasn't exactly sure where the nerves were coming from. We got about an hour of presentation on school procedures, some awkward jokes about lunchtime, and information about how many times a week our kids would go to the library or have music class.

There were a number of questions from parents running the gamut that ultimately led to me completely and unfairly judging which of them I'd actually enjoy hanging out with and which I

think . . . well, not so much (don't lie: you'd do the same thing—
you just wouldn't admit it). It was an odd feeling—kind of like
being back in school for the first time, but not really, and this
time, I'm slightly less socially awkward. Naturally, Danyael and I
sat with the people we knew. Lord knows it is not easy to make
new friends.

A few weeks later, we went to school for a *one-on-one* type
meet & greet/evaluation type of thing. I don't remember doing
this when I was five. Danyael and I walked up to the school's
main entrance and pressed the buzzer. We were allowed in, got
our name tags, and took our seats in the office waiting for whatever would happen next. Next, it turned out, was Julianna getting her picture taken for a *file* followed by the three of us getting
to meet the school's guidance counselor. After that, we got to
meet the school nurse and answer some fun questions, which was
followed by the world-famous you-know-the-drill hearing test.

(right hand up)

(left hand up)

(left hand up)

(pause)

(grin—right hand up)

(etc.)

Once that test was passed, it was back to the waiting area
followed by one of the kindergarten teachers coming to get
Julianna. Off she went, with Ms. M, to do who knows what.
Apparently, they do some block building, skipping (not classes,
but the actual physical movement), and some drawing. Suppos-
edly, they were gauging her skills to help them learn and then
placed the kids in one of the four kindergarten classes at the
school. This ended up being mostly uneventful, slightly surreal,
and all fun (for Julianna).

Skip ahead to a month and a half later.

Kindergarten orientation: kindergartener style. They split
us all up into two groups—you know, one of those "last names

from A-L arrive at 9:30 and M-Z arrive at 10:30" types of deals. Going in, I'm not entirely sure what the plan was or how that day was supposed to work. We milled around the lobby, along with all the other millers, waiting for whatever was going to happen. And then the principal came out and announced that the parents should go [this] way to the cafetorium and the kids go [that] way to a kindergarten classroom.

And that's when the sobbing started. . . .

See, what you have to understand is, I had a really, really difficult time with drop-off when I was in kindergarten. I remember this part of my life vividly. It is possible I've skewed it a bit in the 40 or so years since it happened but I remember being miserable and not allowing my parents to leave. I remember crying endlessly and inconsolably in the elementary school hallway. I don't remember much else.

This time the sobbing was from Julianna. Of course it was her, at least on the outside. I, of course, almost went into convulsions and a minor panic attack as I watched her react as it triggered the memories of what was a very difficult time for me. I sort of got control of myself. She did as well. I don't think I *showed* any of that to her. I watched the guidance counselor—an angel—offer to hold her hand, and then, use the magic words to get her *on board* with the program: "Would you like to hold my clipboard?"

And with that, we were golden, and by we, I mean, she. She went off to do her thing. I went off with the parents to do our thing, which it turns out was the same-ish presentation with the principal as we had about a month and a half ago. I sat there, sort of shaking, the entire time. I sat hoping that Julianna wouldn't experience the same sort of misery I felt when it had been my turn. I sat wondering how I might handle drop-off if it turned out she did. The principal seemed like a nice enough guy, but having heard the presentation before, I found I could use that time more effectively in my own head to wade into the Sea of Anguish. It was tremendous. Even though I saw her walk off sort of happy, I kept my eye on the back of the room waiting for a teacher to bring her in and let us know that *this just wasn't going to work out.*

The presentation ended and we were taken to the classroom to watch the end of whatever it was they had been doing. All smiles. She ran over and gave us hugs. She ran back and got her school T-shirt. She walked out with us, telling us that they had read books, sang songs, and played some [icebreaker] games.

Here's the odd part, though—we all went back to the car and headed to the preschool. Dropping her off felt different that time. It felt more like dropping her off with a babysitter. Her preschool had been great—a truly wonderful experience—and yet now, it felt as though there was something new about to start. Something that I remember hoping she would ultimately love as much as this nerd ultimately, but not right away, did.

She was about to embark on a new adventure and 40 or so years from now when she looks back at those days, I hope the story she tells is the one where she remembers how it was really, really difficult for her daddy to do drop-off in kindergarten.

So as the days went by, leading up to THE day, I stopped sleeping, aged about 10 years, started talking to myself (out loud), had some back issues, grew more grey hair, ate gallons of ice cream, and became a *cat lady*; all the while trying to keep on a happy face on and talk with Julianna about how much fun kindergarten was going to be. We talked about all the great friends she'd make and all the great things she'd learn. Generally speaking, she seemed rather pleased by the whole prospect but I'm no dope . . . I've heard this song before.

THE day rolls around and the plan is set. The school started on a Thursday for Julianna. There are multiple kindergarten classes in her school and the school splits the start up into two days, with half of the kids in each class going each day. This is a nice way, so they say, for the kids to get to meet the teachers and some of the other kids without quite as much craziness. There are four girls from Julianna's preschool who will also attend the same kindergarten but only one will be in her actual class. Two of those girls went on Wednesday and two would be there on Thursday, along with Julianna. We were hopeful that seeing familiar faces might help. Thursday was also a day when our nanny came over to spend the day with Chloe, so that freed up Danyael and I both to go to the first day of school and not have to worry about Chloe. Also, hopefully working in our favor, was Julianna's cousin, who had just started first grade in the same school.

The school's plan was that on day one, you arrived with your kids and waited in a courtyard in front of the school. The courtyard was filled with more nervous energy than Fenway Park would have before a World Series Game seven. There was a lot of side-swaying, sweaty palms, and people who, like me, were on the verge of crying. There also were plenty of teachers and the aforementioned guidance counselor who saved the day last time. Interestingly enough, she came over to say hi. She remembered us. Swell. I told her that I might embarrass myself today, but one day I was likely to be the president of the PTO so she shouldn't hold it against me . . . and also, we might need her help. She told us she would be standing by. The principal then came out and told some jokes and tried to warm up the crowd, all this while I pee in my pants in anticipation.

Then for fun, he was going to say the name of a teacher and then all the students in that teacher's class should line up and *head on in! YEE HAW!* And Julianna started crying, but I was holding it together. Stay strong, Matt.

"Please don't leave me, Mommy."

"Don't leave me, Daddy. I don't want to go in."

The first teacher is called and the first group of kids made their way in, most of whom are reasonably cooperative.

One by one, the other teachers and their respective students are called as the anticipation and anxiety rise. The crying and grasping persisted. I tried to figure out in my head what was going to happen next. I could tell that Julianna's teacher was going to be last. Finally, they call *our* teacher and most of the kids lined up and got going. Julianna, still less than enthusiastic about the whole thing, refused. The guidance counselor came over to assist and together, we decided that one parent at a time, we will hand off. As the class headed in (apparently there is an understanding that this one time, it is better for everyone if a *child is left behind*), most of the parents were now starting to leave—their children having crossed the education threshold. They were all practically celebrating.

"Let's go get some coffee and a scone," I heard one exclaim. What are we, in England?

Danyael and I decided that it was best if I broke off first. I gave Julianna a hug, told her I loved her, and held myself together as she told me during the hug that she loved me, and I walked away.

I didn't look back. Eye contact would have been a disaster. I went straight to the car and hoped for the best. What felt like an hour (but was probably just a minute) later, Danyael got in the car and I decided it was then safe for me to look to the courtyard in the distance.

It was empty. Apparently, Julianna had gone in.

We headed home. About three minutes after we got home, my cell phone rang. Here we go. . . .

Sidebar: my mother would tell you that when I was in kindergarten, she waited outside in her car—that is, once I let her leave—because back then there were no cell phones and what if they needed her and what if I refused to cooperate?

So . . . my cellphone rang and I'm about to get my car keys to head back, but rather than do that, I answer. Of course, it's the guidance counselor. She was calling to tell me that Julianna was smiling and in her classroom. They walked together past her cousin's first-grade class and she got a wave, and that made her feel good. The guidance counselor gave her a book to deliver to her teacher so she could feel like a helper, and that made her even happier. Yada yada, she's fine and sitting in class.

(Deep breath.)

Next—moms and dads were invited to come into class for the last 30 minutes of the first day. We could meet the teachers and have our kids show us around the room. I figured she'd be in tears, but instead she ran over, ear-to-ear smiling, and extremely excited to show us all the things:

- Where her backpack goes (which is slightly bigger than her)
- Her coat hook
- The listening station
- The sink
- The rug for circle time
- Her desk
- Even where the bathroom is—the school had bathrooms attached to each kindergarten classroom so the kids didn't have to travel far when they had to go

She dragged us over to introduce us to her teacher and even told us she made a friend that day.

So that's it? She loved it all. She was very excited to come back tomorrow (she said).

Of course, it got more complicated tomorrow . . . because tomorrow there was no courtyard nonsense. Tomorrow wasn't a dress rehearsal. Tomorrow was a drive-up-to-the-dropoff-circle-and-she-jumps-out day.

Tomorrow arrived, and the plan was it would just be Julianna and me. The day before, after Day 1, we worked on learning how to unbuckle herself and how to open her own car door. She seemed excited to try out these new skills. I didn't fully understand how this was supposed to work at drop-off, but there was a very tight and specific window when kids who weren't arriving by bus were dropped off. We headed out and on the ride over, I was trying to keep the conversation simple, fun, and carefree. I was hoping that the guidance counselor would be in the area to help. I was hoping that there wouldn't be other cars in the drop-off circle that beeped or tried to hurry us if we ran into any problems. I was hoping that it wouldn't be quite as bad as the day before. I was hoping that she'd see a friend she recognizes heading in and that would make it easier.

We turned into the school area and found ourselves in the line of cars waiting to drop their kids off. I told her truthfully that I wasn't exactly sure where I was supposed to drive to and how it would work, but I was sure it would be another fun day.

We saw the circle and I figured out how I thought it was supposed to work. We happened to see some buses pull in and across the way, in one of the buses, Julianna saw her cousin again. This was a good sign. My niece got off the bus and headed on with the stream of kids. Slowly but surely, we made our way up the line. . . .

And then we started to enter the circle . . . here we go . . . deep breath, Matt.

"Okay Julianna, when I stop the car ahead, you can unbuckle."

Our turn. I put the car in park and look back.

"Okie dokie, time to go."

She looked at me. Unbuckled. Hopped out of her seat, and started to open the car door. I had her school bag in the front with me, so I leaned over and pushed the passenger-side front door open. She got her door open, looked back at me with a big *I-did-it* smile, and got out.

She closed her door and moved to the front.

I handed her the backpack and leaned over for a kiss.

I said, "Have a great day. I love you."

She said, "Love you too, Daddy."

She put her backpack on, waved, and started to walk off with the stream of other kids.

There was pressure to keep the cars moving, so I started to slowly move.

She looked back, smiled ear-to-ear, waved, and turned to go in.

And just like that, I had a kindergartener.

CHAPTER NINETEEN

The Death Discussion—Ages 5–6

"Daddy, what's the situation with death?"

I am fortunate to come from a family where people generally live long lives. The first time one of my grandparents passed away was when I was 28, five days before my wedding. I consider myself to be pretty lucky in this regard. I also had a handful of great aunts and uncles who were also alive and well at my wedding.

My wife, Danyael, wasn't quite as lucky. I only got to meet one of her grandparents. We got married in 2007; Julianna was born in 2008; and Chloe was born in 2009. The result of all this timing was that our daughters actually got to meet and spend some time with four great-grandparents, four grandparents, and even a few great-great aunts. It wasn't until Chloe and Julianna were 12 and 13, respectively, that I lost the last of my grandparents and they were 14 and 15 when they lost their first grandparent—Danyael's mother, Deanne. In the intervening years, as various people they knew in some form or another passed away, there were plenty of conversations about death.

When my great-aunt Charlotte passed away, it inspired all sorts of interesting and reasonably difficult discussions with Julianna. Charlotte was really the first *older* person they knew who died. Chloe was five at the time and was about to start kindergarten. She was not particularly interested in these matters, which was fine by me. Julianna was six and about to start first grade. She was enjoying her first summer camp experience, was mildly sensitive about emotional things, and was pretty inquisitive.

To put the sensitivity into context, which I think is relevant for this conversation, here's a quick story from just before Charlotte died: We were on our way to the pool, listening to "Joseph and the Amazing Technicolor Dreamcoat" in the car (musical theater is a thing for us in case that hasn't been apparent). We were just going through it for the first time. I'm not sure if you are familiar with the story, but if you aren't, Google it. We listened to a lot of Broadway showtunes with the girls (deal with it). They loved it. Anyway, the finale, "Any Dream Will Do" came on. We had pulled into the parking lot but the girls wanted to hear the rest of the song. The lyrics talk about Jacob coming to Egypt to reunite with Joseph and his sons and yada yada yada. Happy Ending Land.

Chloe said, "Daddy, Julianna is crying." I turn to the back seat and sure enough, she's quietly crying. I ask why. She tells me that she's crying because she's happy now that she knows—for sure—that Jacob gets to be back with his sons, and in particular Joseph.

"So, this is a happy cry?"

"Yes, but I don't want to listen to this song for a while because I don't want to cry every time."

Okay, so this is the level of emotional sensitivity we're dealing with.

Sidebar: Charlotte was an art lover, both creating and consuming. She didn't have any dependents, so when she passed away, we all visited her apartment and took a few pieces of her art to remember her by. In our house at the time, we had Charlotte paintings in our bedroom and both of the girls' bedrooms.

There was one painting that she had just recently started working on but hadn't finished. It was to be a painting based on a picture of Julianna with my sister's daughter. Unfortunately, she didn't get very far into this piece of work. She hadn't really started drawing my niece yet, but Julianna's outline was there. We recognized it very clearly from the picture on which it is based. To be honest, it was perhaps a bit haunting but also quite beautiful. When you looked at it, if you knew Charlotte, you can almost feel her hand on it. I think it was sort of comforting. It was hanging in Julianna's room. She seemed to really like it, other than occasionally when it started her thinking about Charlotte . . . which led to a conversation with Julianna in her room one night shortly after Charlotte had died. I actually thought she had already been sleeping when out of the blue she asked, *"Daddy, what's the situation with death?"*

"Um . . . What do you mean?"

"Like, what happens with death? How does it work? When does it happen?"

Okay, so here we were. I don't claim to be an expert on children. I'm certainly not professionally trained in this sort of discussion or a licensed anything other than a licensed driver. She brought up these types of questions up before, more frequently around this time, with both Danyael and me and I don't think we had exactly figured out how to comfortably answer.

So that night I just decided to go with it. F*ck it. We'd do it off-the-cuff.

The following were the bits and pieces of what we talked about, in no particular order.

"Well, Julianna, can you tell me two things your heart does?"

"*It moves air around my body.*" Right (sort of/not really). "*It is also how we love.*"

I found my pulse under my neck and put her fingers there. I asked her if she could feel the "bump-bump, bump-bump." She smiled a bit and told me she could. Well, that's my heart, actually working. It is pushing the blood all over my body. The blood carries the oxygen and brings the air all over the place to make sure I'm good to go. I helped her find her own pulse. Another smile. There it is. Her heart is working.

Now that we *knew* how being alive works, we discussed what happens when the heart stops working. While we didn't have to worry about this for a long time (more about this in a bit), there comes a point, a very long time from now, when the heart stops being able to push the air around your body and that's when the death situation happens.

"*So, what happened with Aunt Charlotte? Her eyes opened and then like, they closed really quickly? How does that feel?*"

That's not exactly how it works. I explained that it wasn't painful. That if you could imagine, and again, not something to worry about for a long time, the most peaceful sleep. She closed her eyes for a great sleep and that was it.

"*Okay, so can we go and see her?*"

"Well, we can't see her body."

This brought us into the next phase of the conversation . . . funerals and cemeteries. (Spoiler alert for those worried: She slept great that night—I didn't ruin her—I don't think.)

We talked about what a funeral was and how people get sad because they won't be able to see or touch or hug or laugh or have a conversation with the person who died, but that we spend a lot of time, almost like a party, telling great stories and remembering the great experiences we shared with the person.

We talked about what a cemetery was and how for some people, their bodies were put in this place and that we could always go and visit if we needed a real *place* to see, but that anytime we wanted, Charlotte's spirit would be in Julianna's heart. That she could always think about Charlotte or look at the paintings she now has hanging in her room and smile knowing that some part of Charlotte was with her always.

I told her that it wasn't as important that someone died as it was to enjoy the time that you are alive with that person.

"Well, when are you going to die?"

Nobody really knows that. Like I've said before, I'm pretty lucky to have a lot of healthy people in my family so I used the following:

> "Julianna, I'm your daddy and you know how old I am,
>   right?"
> *"Right."*
> "And who is my daddy?"
> *"Papa."*
> "Is he still alive?"
> *"Yes."*
> "And how old is he?"
> *"Old."*
> "And who is his daddy?"
> *"Great-Grandpa Abe."*
> "And is he still alive?"
> *"Yes."* [foreshadowing]
> "And how old is he?"
> *"Very old."*
> "Right. You shouldn't worry about any of those things."

We didn't discuss that not every story plays out that way. I think the goal was to give her some answers to her questions and make her feel like there was less mystery, while not focusing on the scary or sad parts.

"Well, the next time someone dies, I want us to have a party at our house to remember them."

"Sounds good to me."

She went to sleep shortly after that without fuss. I was sure that the conversations would continue over time. I consider myself to be a pretty logical and science-based thinker. I have always liked to know how things work and why things are the way they are. I think a lot of kids—Julianna included—are like that. There are certainly topics and certain details that are better discussed when they are older, but I tried to put myself in her shoes on this one. I can relate to general fear of the unknown. If there's an explanation to be had, or at least part of an explanation, why not share it appropriately?

At least until she asked this:

"Like, how do your bones get out of your skin after you die?"

Pass?

So back to when Charlotte actually died and how—prior to that, I would spend time thinking about when it was right to talk to my kids about death. Should I wait until someone they knew actually died when it would feel more *acute* or preempt it and perhaps make them more nervous/anxious?

I think the first indication that we were getting close to having the conversation was when Julianna asked at one point, long before Charlotte died, what happened to mosquitoes or bees when they *got squashed*. It was the first time that either of my daughters showed any sign of understanding that there's another *state* beyond what they can see. It wasn't long after that the dots started to connect. If a bug's life can end, can people stop living too?

When I was a kid, my parents, sister, and I would go to my grandmother and grandfather's house every Sunday afternoon. It was a two-family house. Grandma and Grandpa lived in the main unit and Charlotte lived in the other. Over the years, these visits usually involved greetings; some play time; a meal with some combination of my aunts and uncles, my cousins, Charlotte, and various guests; more playing; dialing up Prodigy; watching the Red Sox; playing outside; losing a ball over the neighbor's fence and never getting it because of a mysterious and unseen (but definitely heard) scary dog; and one other thing: I am pretty sure that about 100 percent of the visits involved some sort of craft or project over in Charlotte's house—*every time*. She always had something prepared for the kids. She was always ready for us. She never had kids of her own and I suspect that my father, his two brothers, and his sister would agree with me, my sister, and my five first cousins that Charlotte always treated us like we were all her kids.

The girls (Julianna more than Chloe) would occasionally ask about death around that time. "Daddy, when are you going to be dead?" I think they were starting to understand some of the implications and Danyael and I spent a lot of time reinforcing that even if we weren't physically able to see, hug, or play with that person anymore, it doesn't mean they didn't continue to be alive in our hearts; in our minds. I genuinely believe that it made sense to them.

During a different conversation with Julianna around that time that revolved around her trying to figure out how many birthdays someone can have, she said, "Daddy, what happens when Great-Grandpa Abe [Charlotte's older brother] turns 100?" I knew exactly what she was asking; she was learning about numbers and was trying to wrap her mind around life and setting expectations for herself. My answer was something like, "Well, each year on your birthday your age goes up by one." Danyael and I would both typically redirect into something that focuses more on life rather than death.

Chloe often just listened but didn't have much to say on the matter. She was perhaps too young to understand the impact so she would just let it soak in. We also had planned a trip to New York to visit Danyael's grandmother Minnie. Julianna asked, "Mommy, does Great-Grandma Minnie live with Great-Grandpa Joey?"

"No."

"*Why not?*"

"Great Grandpa Joey isn't living anymore."

"*So, he's dead?*"

"Yes, but he was a wonderful man and he lives in my heart."

Unfortunately, neither my kids nor I ever had the chance to meet him but Julianna followed up with one of her more touching responses as her eyes welled up: "But I miss him."

Like many people who grow old, Charlotte certainly had her share of health problems, but she was probably the most vibrant, full-of-life person I've ever known, literally right up until the end. I don't know if I ever witnessed her doing anything other than smiling, for my entire life. I mean, who is that happy for that much time?

When Charlotte became seriously ill, she was taken to the hospital. Just a few days later, my sister and I visited her there. We knew things weren't good and that she was in an incredible amount of pain and discomfort. Danyael asked the girls to paint pictures so I could take them to her because painting was one of Charlotte's biggest passions. The girls got right to work. My sister's kids did the same.

When my sister and I got to the hospital, Charlotte was asleep, but clearly not comfortable. Two of my cousins also were there. The four of us stood there for a while, letting her sleep. We all thought that waking her up so she knew we were there was a good idea. A nurse helped wake her up. She slowly made eye contact with each of us. We told her that the kids had made pictures for her. I went and got the pictures and held them up so she could get a good look. In perfect Charlotte form, she gave us her classic ear-to-ear, full-of-life, you-just-won-a-million-dollars smile. For that moment, it was literally perfect. She almost immediately fell back asleep.

Charlotte died the next day. When we sat down with the girls that night, Danyael and I decided we'd just tell the girls the truth. They listened as we told them that Great-Aunt Charlotte had died. They listened as we told them that she absolutely loved the pictures they had painted. We told them that even though we wouldn't be seeing her at family gatherings anymore, we'd still have her in our hearts and in our minds and memories. She'd always be with us as long as we shared stories and laughed about all the great times we were lucky enough to spend with her. Following my wife's lead, they both pantomimed locking thoughts away.

Chloe asked, "Daddy, how did she die? Did her heart stop?"

"Girls, it's far less important how she died. What's most important is to always remember how she lived."

Two years later, my grandfather, Abe Brand, died. He was 97 years old and I can't imagine what life would have been like without his influence; without his presence.

We all have starting lines. We have places where the family tree begins. Certainly, I'm aware that before my grandfather, there were his parents and other people, but I never knew any of them. For me, he is at my starting line, and while not alone there, he has always represented a huge part of my origin story.

For my kids, he was slightly more out of reach, slightly harder to understand, but they too will likely look back and view him as a presence on their starting line as well. Julianna was just about 8 and Chloe was just about 7 when he passed away.

He is my name. Abraham Brand. His initials: A & B. The beginning.

To my kids, he had been their dad's dad's dad. That's pretty far removed from their ability to comprehend the family tree. When his health took its final turn for the worse, many of the people in our family were going to visit him in the hospital and eventually in hospice. The kids had known the whole time that he was sick and not doing well, but that he was comfortable and had his family around him. Each morning, for those last few days, in her normal matter-of-fact way, Chloe has asked me if Great-Grandpa Abe had died yet. Julianna would listen for the answer intently but didn't say much. Chloe was a bit more analytical while Julianna was a bit more emotional. After my previous visit, I got home around 8:30 at night and the girls had been in bed. I heard Julianna call down the stairs to me right when I came in the house: "Dad, how is Great-Grandpa doing?"

So, they knew. We didn't hide what was going on and answered any questions they had. Shortly after he had passed, at dinner, Danyael and I were sharing funny stories about times with their great-grandpa. She told them about the story of the first time she met him at a family dinner and how legend has it that after— in his car ride home—he expressed that he was in love with her to my father. Chloe asked, "Does that mean he's going to marry you, Mommy?"

Julianna then said, "He was also so kind."

It's hard to put my relationship with him into words. For some people, I perhaps give the impression that I'm loud. For those who know me well, you know I actually prefer quiet. Some of my best times with him were quiet ones. We didn't need to talk. It was enough to be nearby. When we were in a conversation, it was often about business. I'm not sure there are (or were) many 97-year-olds as progressive as he was. I think my professional life was a pretty foreign concept to him at first. He started his business 64 years earlier and went to work—practically and literally—up until the end.

In those same 64 years, it's feasible that I'll have 32 jobs. I work in the tech startup space. It is a different world, but one that over the years, Grandpa and I had lots of conversations about. I think he was troubled by the volatility of it all at first and then later, fascinated by the excitement. He was always happy to talk about work.

In one of my favorite pictures of him from the last Thanksgiving he was with us, he was holding court with his four great-grandchildren. It might be the only time I've seen all four so completely engrossed in a conversation at the same time. They were discussing what they were going to be when they grew up. I think he was incredibly proud of what he created. At many of these large family events, he would hold court in one form or another, often attempting to take credit for *creating* the entire family tree. The tree of people who were present would often include friends, in-laws, and a variety of people who were not at all related—but it didn't matter. The amazing thing is that he was always quiet and humble but he wore his pride on his sleeve.

It was this balance of humility, pride, and ambition that I think I take as the greatest lesson from him. Too much pride can lead to too much ego. Too much ambition can lead to carelessness. He was the perfect balance. This balance is where I like to live my life; it is where I'd like my kids to live theirs.

I consider myself incredibly fortunate to have had him in my life for as long as I did. I spent a lot of time with him over the last week and a half of his life and while he slept for almost all of it, the last time I said something to him that he responded to, in the hospital, it went like this (which if you knew both of us, you might appreciate a bit more):

> "Hey Grandpa, I'm going to come back later and take you out drinking."
> GRANDPA: [laughing] "Okay."

Simple and perfect.

There are so many things that aren't certain about life, but here's one that is: while he won't be walking among us any longer, he'll always walk with us.

Let's keep the good times rolling. The girls are now 13 and 14.

Each summer, when I was a kid and before I started going to overnight camp, my family would go to Cape Cod for two weeks for vacation. My sister and I, along with my parents and my mother's parents (Bubbie and Zadie), made up the core group of vacationers. We would get visitors from other parts of the family over the course of our stay. We stayed in different towns over the years.

The last time I can remember going, I was probably nine years old. My memories for those trips are more than 35 years old at this point. I don't remember every moment of every trip, but for those that I do remember, they are as vivid today as they were back then.

For multiple summers we stayed in Wellfleet, which is a small town that sits pretty high up on Cape Cod. It is about 15 miles south of Provincetown (the town all the way at the end of the Cape). We stayed in this small cabin that was, frankly, gross. I remember waking up one night and finding an army of ants on my pillow. I remember sitting in the kitchen sink to take a bath. The beauty of this place wasn't the inside though; it was its proximity to the ocean.

From this cabin, we'd walk down this long sand path framed by tall grass that, given my height at the time, came up to my neck. There were giant sandpits that I could fall down (on purpose) and just play for hours. The sand at the bottom of these pits was always quite a bit cooler on my feet than the rest of the beach.

We spent a lot of time on the beach on those visits. There wasn't much else to do in that place. I've never been a big fan of swimming and as such, not a huge fan of the ocean. We would go to the beach, all of us carrying something. I would drag this inflatable boat with the rope around it down the sandy path all the way to the ocean. My Bubbie would have one of those low-to-the-ground beach chairs. We would get to the beach and she would plant her chair about one foot from the edge of the water. She would strap the boat's rope around one of the chair's legs and then plant me in the boat, and her in the chair. I'd sit in that boat for what felt like hours, gently rocking in the first eight inches of the ocean. I don't remember if we talked about anything during that time. I don't remember if I had any toys with me or if she was doing anything other than being my boat's anchor. I just remember sitting in the boat, on the edge of the ocean, hoping she wouldn't let me drift off to Portugal, or wherever the ocean would take me.

Some other time, she and my Zadie took my sister and me on a trip to Provincetown. They took us to this cute little gift shop/general store type of place. Bubbie bought me a Rubik's Cube. There was something odd about this particular cube though. It was in a box that was all black. At the time of purchase, I wasn't sure why, but The Bubster (as I liked to call her) paid for it and back to the car we went. Zadie was driving (slowly: that was his signature move). While Bubbie did have her driver's license, I don't ever recall being in a car with her in the driver's seat (and if she ever was, I'm reasonably sure she wouldn't have been able to see over the steering wheel without a phone book to sit on).

I opened the box of the Rubik's Cube and much to my surprise, it wasn't covered in the standard colors. Each of the six sides were emblazoned with a picture of a different—and very naked—man.

I asked her what kind of Rubik's Cube this was? She casually took it from me and I've not seen it since. A few years ago, and many years after the incident, I got her a *standard* Rubik's Cube as a gift. She put it on her TV stand as a reminder.

Then there was the time in a different Cape Cod town—Brewster, I believe—where we stayed in a house that had its very own small fishing dock on a small lake in the backyard. The Bubster would sit in her chair (probably the same chair from the beach) on the dock while I learned how to fish. One day we were out there fishing and my mother was out there with us, wearing some [ugly] green socks. I went to cast my fishing line and, on the backswing, got it stuck on one of my mother's socks. Panic ensued. The Bubster sprang into action to try to extricate the hook from the sock but in attempting to do so, hooked her own finger. Fortunately for my mother (and the rest of us who had to suffer her wearing those green socks), we were able to get the sock off, cut the line, and head to the emergency room. The Bubster was attached to my mother's green sock via my fishing hook, laughing the whole time.

Then, there was the infamous whale watch. Given my general distaste for the ocean, you'd think it wouldn't be my thing, but I had always been fascinated with whales so that outweighed whatever ocean trepidation I had. My mother, The Bubster, and I were the only three from the group who wanted to go. Bubbie was dressed with her white shoes and her Sophia Petrillo bag like she was on her way, with "The Golden Girls," via the "Love Boat," to "Gilligan's Island." Zadie dropped us off at the boat dock. I didn't realize what a time commitment it was. I believe it was probably three hours of boating out followed by 20 to 30 minutes of viewing, and then three hours back. While still in the harbor, we were sitting in the inside cabin of the boat and The Bubster realized that coffee was being sold for $0.05 a cup (callback). What a bargain! "Matty," she would call me, "Go get me a cuppa coffee." I think I probably went back four or five times while in the harbor. This particular whale watch was sparsely attended, and it's a good thing. . . .

Once we exited the harbor, the real ocean happened—and by that, I mean, very choppy waters. It wasn't long before those white shoes The Bubster was wearing looked more like the green socks my mother was wearing for the great fishing incident. I don't think she was able to stand up the entire boat ride. I'm talking nonstop seasickness. Eventually we reached calm waters for the actual viewing of whales. Aside from a few crew members, I was the only passenger outside the boat cabin area looking at the whales. I remember calling to my mother and The Bubster that the whales were breaching and hoping that someone would join me in the excitement. Alas, The Bubster was still repainting her shoes and my mother was attempting to find solace in the palms of her hands. Hey, good news everyone—three more hours of rough waters to get back to shore.

Needless to say, when we got back, The Bubster walked with us back to Zadie's waiting car—barefoot—and declared that this whale watch would be a once-in-a-lifetime kind of thing.

The Bubster was the last of my grandparents to pass away and I truly think she'd rather us laugh about ridiculous stories involving fishing hooks attached to socks and whale watch coffee than anything else. She was the funniest person I have ever known. Everything about my sense of humor comes from her. She was proud and loud and warm and open-minded and progressive—and so hilarious.

My mother would tell the following story better, but I'll give it a try. The Bubster used to manage a women's lingerie store in Malden (where she lived) called Lady Grace. Apparently, people would come from all over the country to have her fit them for bras. At some point, she started receiving customers who were men as well. Her store didn't have a men's dressing room though, so they had to use the next best thing—a storage closet. The men would try things on, with her waiting outside, and impatiently calling for them to *come out of the closet*. She apparently liked to take credit for coining that phrase.

You know that feeling you get after you hear a great joke? You get that feeling that you need to tell someone else; you need to share it. I don't think many of us have a grandmother on speed dial for that. Well, I did.

"Bubster, sit down for this one . . ."

I'd tell her a dirty joke and she would always make this overdramatic gasping sound, like she was shocked that her grandson would tell her such disgusting things. She would then often start cackling and then occasionally claim that the joke may have made her pee in her pants, just a little.

It wasn't all jokes though; just mostly. The other times we would speak, she wanted to talk about the Red Sox, what I thought about whatever was going on in national politics, our pets, or how my kids were doing. Nothing was ever SO serious. Nothing was too big or too small to talk about. Nothing was out of bounds.

A life like hers is hard to come by and I think you'd have been lucky to have her in your life for even a fraction of what I had. Her life was long, full, and filled with love, laughter, family, and happiness.

When we found out that she was nearing the end, my sister and I made a trip to the hospital to visit (this has been a common theme). You never really know what you're going to experience on those types of visits. In my experience, the person I'm visiting is usually sleeping. We went into her room and she was awake. She gave us a big smile. We gave her updates on what was going on in our worlds and relayed the message that our kids said hi and that they loved her. I ran down my list of normal topics we like to cover, including telling her that the Yankees had lost the night before in Game 2 of the American League Championship Series. She watched and supported the Red Sox like they were her religion—a passion that grew in Zadie's later years and a connection she kept with him until his death right before my wedding in 2007.

She responded with an excited, "Oh, great!"

Even in these moments, she liked to keep things light.

As we said our goodbyes and started to leave, I looked back and asked her one more question, "Bub, be honest, I'm the best looking in the family, right?"

She's never given me a straight answer on this question when I've asked before but this time . . .

"Absolutely!"

I always knew it. I said I loved her and continued to walk out.
She replied, "I love you more!"

I'm not so sure about that last one.

Jump a bit ahead now—Julianna is 15 and Chloe is 14.

In September of 2023, Danyael's mother—my daughters'
grandmother—Grandma Didi (Deanne), passed away. She is
the first of my daughters' grandparents to die. With permission
from Danyael, the following is the speech I gave at the funeral:

> I am equal parts sad and honored to be speaking today.
> When my wife asked me to speak on behalf of her, her
> sister, brother, and father, I was a bit nervous that I'd be
> able to properly represent them and also properly honor
> Grandma Didi. Here goes.
>
> My Danyael (my wife) and I met in 1992 but didn't
> really connect until 2005. Most people meet their future
> in-laws after they've been dating for a while but not me.
> I met Barry, my now father-in-law, before Danyael and
> I reconnected and I met Grandma Didi on Friday, July
> 1st, 2005, at the crossroads at Camp Tevya. Danyael was
> with her and this would also become the beginning of
> my courtship with Danyael. I didn't spend much time
> with Deanne at that time because it was about 30 sec-
> onds later that she ran off to join a group of campers
> doing a yoga class.
>
> There were two things I learned fairly quickly that were
> good signs for Danyael and me: First, she and her mother
> share a birthday, just like I do with my mother. The other:
> Danyael and her mother shared a love for musical theater.
> Danyael's favorite musical is "A Chorus Line."
>
> *Kiss today goodbye*
> *The sweetness and the sorrow*
> *Wish me luck, the same to you*

But I can't regret
What I did for love, what I did for love

Deanne was a fiercely loyal and supportive partner to Barry. They were married for 60 incredible years. The devotion and dedication to her "Ben" is something that gives me inspiration in my relative to them, "new" marriage, coming up on 18 years. She had three incredibly loving, and very different children who she adored. She had three incredibly loving, and very different grandchildren who she also adored. Michael, Larissa, Rafel, myself, Burt, Jayne, Alicia, Willa, Judy, Rosanne, Mia, Shea, and countless other family, friends, and neighbors. I don't even know some of those people but I guarantee she adored you too. I think I can speak for all of us and say that the feeling was mutual.

I never got to meet her father Joe, Grandpa Joey as I've heard him spoken about, or her brother Harold, and when I met her mother, Minnie, she had already suffered a severe stroke and was only able to say the words, "I can't talk." Amazingly though, Deanne and Minnie continued to have a wonderful relationship because of Deanne's desire and ability to nurture and Minnie's strength and perseverance, something she certainly passed down to her daughter. It makes me smile to imagine that right now, Deanne, Harold, Joe, and Minnie are all probably sitting around a table, like they used to in the one-bedroom Bronx home she grew up in, happily reconnecting and catching up with each other. I imagine Minnie saying to Deanne, "I can talk."

Look, my eyes are dry
The gift was ours to borrow
It's as if we always knew
And I won't forget what she did for love

I've only known her for 18 years so I can't speak to the many experiences before our time together. I have heard stories, however, about visits to Ziggy's house, her time working at the Sports Connection as a fitness instructor, working at the Great Neck Arts Center where she created a film series, Plain Jayne's, and how she used to sell sweaters out of the back of her car with her friend Sheila, accepting cash only (there was no Venmo then).

I'm not going to get into it here but there was also the bus ride to Cortland [N.Y.], where she met Barry but didn't fall in love with him until she saw him in the "infamous" red bathing suit.

Gone
Love is never gone
As we travel on
Love's what we'll remember

As a wife, mother, grandmother, and friend, she was always interested in what was going on in your life. She would always try to find ways to connect "on your terms." When we first started getting to know each other, she would ask me about the New England "Patriots" even though I'm fairly certain she didn't care or know anything at all about football. Each time I wrote on my blog, I was guaranteed to get a message from her about a week or two later telling me how much she enjoyed it. She was always so interested in what was going on in my daughters' lives. She had such a diverse set of skills and interests, never settling for just one or two hobbies, and always fashionable. Deanne was up for anything.

Kiss today goodbye
And point me toward tomorrow
We did what we had to do

Won't forget, can't regret
What she did for love

The way I knew her the most was as a grandmother for my daughters. I will always fondly remember the times I would see her sitting on the floor at our home or hers, playing with little Smurf toys or doing a craft with Julianna and Chloe . . . usually with a giant pair of garden sheers next to her, because she had often just come from gardening—one of her many passions. She and Barry would usually arrive around midday when they would come to visit us in Massachusetts. Usually, I'd be at work at this time. On countless occasions, I would arrive home and see her zipping around the yard, with dirt on her knees, sheers in one hand, and some sort of dangling plant in the other hand. The first few times I witnessed this, I doubted her gardening and pruning skills, particularly when she would cut a 6-foot-tall arborvitae tree down by 75 percent. I'd ask Danyael, "Doesn't that seem a little drastic?" It turns out she knew what she was doing because every time, that tree would come back stronger than it was before. She nurtured those around her like she nurtured plants.

Deanne was deeply connected to Israel and to Judaism. One of my favorite traditions that Jewish people like to do is to plant a tree. That planting represents the circle of life: A tree grows, it loses its fruit and leaves, and comes back again the next season. It nurtures and nourishes constantly, just like Deanne. I would encourage everyone, when you're next at home, to plant something in your yard in Deanne's honor. You know if she was at your home, she'd be doing it for you.

Nat King Cole's song "Nature Boy" has a lyric that I think best represents Deanne's life: "The greatest thing

you'll ever learn is just to love and be loved in return."
While she may not be with us physically anymore and
we will certainly miss her, she'll always be with us in our
hearts. Our stories and memories aren't things we will
or could ever forget.

Love is never gone
As we travel on
Love's what we'll remember.

CHAPTER TWENTY

Good Riddance—Age 7

Obviously, I've known Chloe for essentially 100 percent of her life. When she was an infant, I was a summer camp director. Less than one and a half months after she was born, I moved up to camp for the summer. As a result, it took me longer than I would have liked to really develop a connection with her. I doubt she felt it the way I did, but it wore on me enough that I ultimately left that job and went back into the startup world (which is still very time-consuming but generally doesn't involve me being away for three months in a row in a 24/7 job).

Anyhow, in the years since, I feel like we've remedied that connection and then some. I feel like we know each other pretty well at this point.

In the spring of 2016, we added two new members to our family: Willie and Charlie. They were kittens we rescued. At the time, they rounded out our farm at two parents, two kids, one dog (Cassie, a Mini Labradoodle who was two years old at the time), and two cats. One of the things that I mentioned earlier in the book about Chloe and Julianna—but now had living proof—is how the differences between cats and dogs are similar to the differences between Chloe and Julianna.

So, we know Chloe is like a cat (in terms of her personality). Let's just say, as an example, Julianna was in bed and asked me if I could go get her a book from her bookshelf. If I did it, she'd thank me profusely and tell me how awesome I was. If Chloe had been the one asking, when I brought her the book, she would have either been reading something else and ignoring me or would have greeted me with, "What took you so long?"

With Chloe, you must work for it. Her love and affection is earned, but once you get it, she won't leave you alone. I considered it a challenge. She loved playing with friends but was also incredibly happy to just play by herself. She regularly played with LEGO sets—some that she would have built a year earlier and were still intact—for hours by herself. At bedtime, she would occasionally dismiss me from the room so she could get back to the book she was reading. Julianna would welcome my company for the entire night.

Some of my favorite times with Chloe were when we were just sitting near each other, quietly doing our own things. For instance, there were times when she would be playing with Lego blocks and I'd ask if she minded if I sit in the room near her. I offered to play if she wanted but many times, she just seemed happy to have me nearby. Sometimes in the car, when it's just the two of us, we'll listen to music without any conversation and we're both happy about that.

And she's so funny. Her sense of humor really developed around when she was seven-ish, particularly as it related to her ability to understand—and occasionally even express—sarcasm. Her wit is sharp and biting.

I hope the people who share a house with me don't take this the wrong way, but the way I see it, of everyone in my family, she might get my sense of humor the most. She knows exactly when I am joking and is a willing participant in my nonsense. She has become my comedic partner in crime.

Julianna has a good sense of humor too, but it's different. Her comedy didn't come quite as naturally, not for lack of trying, but at the ripe age of eight, she was telling jokes that end with "#dad-joke" and using air quotes like she was motivational speaker Matt Foley.

With Chloe, it was effortless—and her laugh, the real one, has always been intoxicating.

Julianna liked to dance, sing, and perform for people. Chloe is mostly happy to keep to herself. She enjoys, to this day, her quiet and alone time. These are differences I have always loved about them. These differences have allowed them to follow their own paths without conflict or competition (most of the time).

One weekend, we took the girls to a local community theater musical with middle school-aged kids. There was no food allowed in the auditorium. This was our first trip to a *big play* as a family. At intermission, the girls and I went out and got a snack. Julianna chose Cheetos. Chloe chose Skittles. When Julianna finished devouring hers, she went back in to sit with Danyael. Chloe and I sat out in the lobby for five more minutes, just people-watching. She had about half the bag of Skittles left when we went back to our seats so I put the bag in my jacket pocket for later.

During the car ride home after the show, Julianna brought up a story about the time period between when she got back to her seat and when Chloe and I got back to ours. The people sitting in front of us (a mom and a few sons) had a discussion about tasking the son with buying—you guessed it—Skittles, but the concession people were all out. He came back empty-handed. Apparently, before he went on his failed mission, the mom had told him that even though there was no food allowed in the auditorium, he should just sneak it in. This was cause for alarm with Julianna (a consummate rule-follower). If only she knew. . . .

Shortly after the second act started, I reached into my pocket and quietly pulled a few Skittles out. I reached over the armrest and put one in Chloe's hand. She didn't look at me. She hadn't asked. She just closed her fingers around it and then put it in her mouth. No words exchanged. For the rest of the second act, I smuggled Skittles to her.

While Julianna was telling her story, I made eye contact with Chloe in the rear-view mirror. She just barely winked at me. She just barely smiled. We both knew what we had gotten away with—together. We were Skittles fugitives; accessories to the greatest crime in musical theater history.

We have not spoken about it since.

Occasionally, the girls would write notes to my wife and me while they were in bed. I would usually see the notes when I'd go to check on the girls after they were asleep or the following morning. Here is what one of the notes from Chloe said: "Dad – I love you and I want to say goodnight. (and good ridance)" [sic]

I basically pissed my pants laughing when I saw this—and repeatedly throughout the night. The next morning, I asked her what "good riddance" meant. She said she didn't know but had heard it before. I told her that it basically meant, "I don't want to see you ever again." Rather than being mortified about what she had said to me, she started laughing. It took her no time to understand how funny it was, particularly after saying, "I love you and goodnight."

I drove her to elementary school that morning (Julianna was sick, so wasn't with us). This is the same school drop-off that we'd been doing for years. We waited in the line of cars and eventually got into the traffic circle that abutted the front entrance area of the school. When she walked off from my car, I waited for her to get a far enough distance away and into the thick of other kids heading into school for the day along with a few teachers and one custodian. I wanted to make sure that people could hear me yell, "Hey, Chloe, I love you and good riddance!"

She turned around, already with a giant smile on her face, understanding exactly what I meant.

CHAPTER TWENTY-ONE

Waiting at the Mailbox—Age 8

The day camp experience is very different than the overnight (residential) camp experience. At day camp you get on the bus in the morning, spend the day doing all sorts of sports and crafts and swimming activities, and then get on a bus and go home in the afternoon. With overnight camp, you get dropped off on Day One and ... peace out. See you in three and a half weeks (or seven).

In 1983, I started going to a day camp called Camp Simchah. That was fun, but the best was yet to come for me. In 1988, my parents dropped me off at an overnight camp in New Hampshire called Camp Tevya. I was 10, about to turn 11. While I'd love to go into my whole camp story, for the sake of your sanity—and mine—I'll do the summary timeline:

- 1988—Start as a camper
- 1992—Last year as a camper
- 1993—counselor-in-training summer
- 1994–1999—counselor

- 2001—assistant head counselor and a variety of other things
- 2002—head counselor (long story)
- 2004—variety of administrative jobs
- 2005—head counselor (the summer I reconnected with my now wife, Danyael, at camp)
- 2009–2010—Director (Julianna was just over one year old when I started, Chloe was three months old)

So, Julianna took her first steps at this camp while I was the director. She ate many meals and slept many nights at camp. She has been in the lake, and done arts and crafts. Many of the adults who worked at camp knew her and many of the kids who were campers at that time became counselors by the time she started going.

The summer before she was to attend camp for the first time, we went up to do a formal tour of camp. The camp does this each summer so families considering sending their children to camp can come and see how it all works. In my years working at camp, I have given many of these tours. This was the first time I really made a conscious decision to step back and I tried to let the experience be Julianna's. She was pretty excited about the prospects of coming to camp after that tour. Not too long after that, camp had a *try-out* day where any kids who wanted to could come and do some camp activities and get a feel for what a *day-in-the-life* might feel like. The parents were split off while the kids participated in activities. I remember Julianna running up to me a few hours later, with a cookie she baked for me, saying, "Dad, I'm coming to camp next summer."

One more time, "Dad, I'm coming to camp next summer."

And so the countdown began. . . .

Was I a bit nervous? Sure. She would be entering third grade in the approaching fall. That's pretty much the youngest age to come to camp and it was younger than I was when I started going.

Was she nervous? Sure. She told me as much not long before camp started: "I know you and Mom loved it and so I'm sure I will, too."

Leading up to the summer, we would talk periodically—but not constantly—about camp. We asked what she was nervous about and what she was excited about. We reminded her that she would know a ton of the grown-ups at camp and a ton of other kids (including one of her first cousins who was also starting that summer). She helped us with gathering things to pack. She helped make *elective activity* camp choices like *Jazzy Jewelry*, ceramics, and newcomb (like volleyball but you catch and throw the ball instead of hitting it). She went on playdates with other new kids and we all went to the new camper orientation that's held each spring.

I have watched literally thousands of kids go to camp. I used to regularly speak at camp conferences and have visited many camps around the region. At that point in time, I had been involved in the camping world for close to 30 years in one form or another. Five of the years I spent as a counselor were with the youngest age group. This was always the group that had the highest percentage of new campers. This was also the age group that Julianna was starting in. Yada yada yada . . . I had plenty of formal experience with this stuff, and I knew more about this than probably anything else in my life.

But this time was different. We had never been away from each other for this long. It's an odd thing to miss someone so much, so soon, before she's even gone, while at the same time being so incredibly excited for her to start that part of her journey. I knew what would happen next.

She would make the best friends in the world. She would learn a ton about living independently. She would never spend a whole summer at home with me again because she would love camp so much, that next summer she'll go for seven weeks and she will keep going until she can become a counselor, which will take her all the way through college graduation.

Or . . . her story would be different, and here's the key: It was going to be *her* story now and not only was I completely okay with that (as crazy as I—and that—might seem), but I couldn't wait to read it.

We were packing for camp, all of us, both literally and emotionally because . . . it was for three and a half weeks. . . .

And then I found myself waiting at the mailbox, both figuratively and literally, because that's how I would know.

We dropped Julianna off at overnight camp. Assuming that first day went well, she would have a first day of camp for many summers to come, but that day was the *first* first day. That day was the day when it all started. Of course, she had been to day camp before but that day, well, it was a whole different ball game.

Here's how it all went.

For the first few weeks in the spring (months), we'd been preparing for camp. We had a space in the house reserved for collecting all the things we needed: sheets, pillow, towels, battery-powered fans, flashlights, books, floor mat, toiletries basket holder thingy, etc. As we approached Day One, things started to come together, mostly because Danyael is ultra prepared. We included Julianna in the packing process quite a bit over that period of time, so she not only could feel some ownership in the process but also so she knew where everything was that she was taking.

As we neared Day One, she would tell us in passing that she was nervous, but excited. She had been singing the camp songs that she already knew to the point where even I, a diehard camp person, had to ask her to take a break. The night before camp started, we let her choose the dinner she'd like before she left. She chose blueberry blintzes (she didn't know this but that choice was always my favorite camp meal).

Over that time, we tried to talk about all the exciting things she would experience at camp, acknowledge the things that were making her nervous, and answer any and all questions—all while trying to not be too overwhelming.

Three and a half weeks is a short amount of time relative to, let's say, the number of years the Earth has been here. But to a kid—and to me as a father—that's a tremendously long time. I'd never been apart from my kids for more than three or four days and even then, we could talk on the phone or FaceTime. Each of those times, Danyael or some other family had been with them. Each of those times, Chloe was with her too, so they at least had each other. So, this day was going to be weird.

I have participated in many opening days at camp, in many different roles ranging from nonattending sibling (when I was too young to go, but my sister was going) all the way to director of the camp. Until that day, there was one role I hadn't experienced—parent.

You know that first time you leave your baby with a sitter for a few hours so you can go out on a date night? That urge to constantly check in and make sure everything is okay? It felt, at that moment, quite a bit like the babysitter experience, except at camp, it's not for two or three hours. In that case, it's more like 624 hours, give or take. In that case, I won't be texting with the babysitter or FaceTiming. In that case, I've put my trust, all of it, in the camp and its staff to guide Julianna—and ultimately Chloe—on this journey.

The night before camp, we let the girls have one of their *sleepovers*. They loved sleeping together but usually kept each other up, probably too late, particularly before an epic day. I could see the nervousness creep in a tiny bit with Julianna at bedtime. She knew this was the last night at home for a bit.

The morning of drop-off, we woke up at 6:30. Julianna took a shower, ate breakfast, and did some final packing. We hit the road.

We met up with my sister and her family and formed a caravan so we could arrive at camp together, unpack at the same time (neighboring cabins), and leave together. The four parents decided this was the best option to maximize emotional stability for all parties. The drive took just over an hour.

We waited in the car line to get into camp along with over 300 other camper families and before we got out, we were greeted by many familiar faces. Several adults who worked at camp had known Julianna since she was a baby, which was certainly comforting for us and I think also for Julianna, even if she didn't necessarily remember everyone. She was a little tense at this point, but otherwise, it was business as usual.

We drove over to her assigned cabin, which would have 12 girls and four counselors (a great ratio) and parked the car. Julianna led the way—walking with Chloe—with Danyael and I just behind, as we headed into the cabin. Once inside, it was greetings and introductions from her counselors. Part of the fun of opening day is finding out who your counselors are. The counselors were all very friendly and very warm. They made an effort to meet not only Julianna but also Danyael and me, and even Chloe.

There were just two other girls moving in at the same time. In short order, the cabin would be filled. We found out which bed was Julianna's (they are assigned in advance). She was right next to a counselor, which got a favorable reaction from all of us. Out to the car the four of us went, along with some of the counselors—who are responsible for helping all the kids move in—to unload. We got everything in and Julianna started to unpack with the help of her counselors.

Parents have a tendency to overdo it with the unpacking. In my *professional camp experience*, and I'm certainly not the only one who would say this, it is much better to let the kid do it with counselors rather than the parents doing it for them. If her parents did all the unpacking for her, she wouldn't know where anything was. Similar to the packing, if she unpacked herself, she had that much more ownership of the process. It's also a great way to keep busy and not think about what's about to happen. . . .

She made her bed, with the help of a counselor, and in a fairly shocking plot twist, Chloe. Chloe wouldn't help her *mess up* her room at home if I paid her, so when she started helping make the bed, without being asked, it was a fairly resounding signal—this shit is for real.

Danyael and I helped a little (probably a little too much—but resisting is difficult) but for the most part, sort of stood around not wanting to leave, all the while desperately wanting to leave. We made small talk with the counselors, similar to how you made small talk with the babysitter about the 1,000,000 things they *needed* to know. We communicated with my sister to make sure were still on track to leave at the same time. Julianna was actively helping but started to get a bit quiet. She knew what was coming.

Periodically, other people were coming in to say hi to her and to us. These were older kids whom she knew from home, or adults with whom Danyael and I went to this very camp. Generally, it was nice to see so many friendly faces, but I was not particularly interested in socializing. I, like Julianna, knew what was coming.

No tears yet.

For years I've spoken to counselors, in the week leading up to camp during staff training, about how crazy it is that parents will leave their children at camp, with these counselors—a group of people who, for the most part, they don't know—full-time for three and a half weeks at a time (seven if you stay the whole summer). *It's nuts.* Could you imagine leaving your kid alone with a babysitter for three and a half weeks when they were eight?

But here's the thing, I've used the babysitter as a point of reference a bunch of times here because that's the closest comparison.

It's not actually like that at camp. The counselors are like surrogate parents. So far, we have done the best we can to set up our kids to be strong, confident, smart, and maybe a little resilient. We've set them up, as far as we know, to be good citizens, do nice things, share, not swear (yet), and not smoke crack. That job, at least for those next few weeks, was someone else's responsibility.

So, it was time to leave. We had stalled as much as we could. A few pictures and then hugs for everyone. Chloe and Danyael got into the car, and I walked her back into her cabin so her counselors could take over when the tears started (for her—and maybe for others). And then the surprise happened—*no tears.* She told me to look at the cabin window from the outside as I was getting in the car.

I did.

She was there, waving.

"Bye, Dad."

We knew we would see photos online that the camp posts daily. We knew we would send letters, both online and via snail mail. She would hear from us.

She would write to us, too. Campers are required to write a letter home at least three times a week.

And with that, I knew I'd be standing at the top of our driveway, by the mailbox, waiting to get a letter from her, telling me what my brain already knew, but my heart wouldn't mind being reassured about. . . .

"Dad, I'm too busy having fun to write. Everything's great."

CHAPTER TWENTY-TWO

Good Conversations—Age 9

During the winter of the year when Chloe was nine, our family went on a weekend trip to New York City. In "Chevy Chase Vacation" style, the four of us, along with my sister, her family, and our parents all piled into a rented twelve-passenger van and hit the road.

The ride down was uneventful, relatively speaking. We arrived on a Friday afternoon, had a mid-afternoon lunch-dinner type situation, and then headed for the hotel to check in.

The next day, we went for a great walk on the High Line and then to lunch. We had tickets for all of us to see a matinee showing of "Jersey Boys" that everyone was excited for. Danyael and I have always been huge fans of musical theater. When we were dating, she was living in New York City and I was living in Boston. We would visit each other every other weekend, alternating locations. Since we both love theater, that was a pretty regular activity during the New York visits. Both Julianna and Chloe had started to enjoy seeing musicals.

The first Broadway show they saw was "School of Rock" and it was a perfect first for them. The actors were mostly kids and the kids all played their own musical instruments. It was a funny and cool show with catchy music. We loved the show and took the kids to the stage door after the show so they could hopefully see some of the actors up close—maybe even get some autographs. They got to say "Hi" to most of the main characters, take some pictures, and get a bunch of signatures on their Playbills.

After that first show, we saw some others, including "Hamilton" in Boston, where they managed to get autographs from almost every main character. So, it was pretty common for us, whenever we saw a show, to wait around afterward to see if we could meet anyone. This brings us to "Jersey Boys." That show has been around a while and was then playing in a just-off-Broadway theater. After the show, which the girls loved (for more than just the exhaustive use of the word *fuck*), we waited near a door we thought might yield some cast members. It happened to be right near the coat check.

[Pause]

I'm about to tell you the part of a story about a challenging conversation I had with Chloe who was nine at the time. In my opinion, it's a great conversation and exploration of a topic that is tricky for a lot of people. As a parent and a human, I am always learning. I certainly don't always say the right thing and I definitely make mistakes. I am not afraid of going through and sharing that process. It sometimes feels like in our society, you have to get something exactly right or you might be portrayed as being a terrible person. That's just not how I see it. Danyael and I have never shied away from challenging conversations and this was no different. I'm proud to have daughters who are willing to ask questions—even if they make some people uncomfortable—in the service of learning.

[Unpause]

The girls managed to meet a few cast members who were incredibly gracious—to stop and chat for a few minutes and sign their programs. It turns out though, that this stage door encounter was not the most interesting thing that happened that afternoon. . . .

Chloe tapped me on the arm, gestured for me to look over to the coat check, and whispered, "Is that a transgender person?"

Well, I didn't see that coming. We'd never had that conversation and I wasn't even sure where she had learned the word. I looked over to where she was looking and answered that I wasn't sure. Before we could get into any more of a conversation, she got distracted by more cast members and then with her cousins, sister, and everyone else standing around—I didn't feel like it was a good time to bring it up again.

Skip ahead a few hours to dinner and all 10 of us were at a long table. I was sitting in the middle and Chloe was on my immediate left (a place that she would often be when we went to a restaurant). During the meal she leaned over—unprompted—and quietly said, "How does being transgender work?"

It turned out that we were going to have this conversation right then. She showed no signs of judgement or concern in her voice or eyes. She was wondering about something that is frankly pretty confusing for a lot of people. I certainly didn't (and don't) know all the answers on that topic and I didn't feel at all properly prepared to answer whatever questions she had. I was—however—determined to allow the conversation and to be as honest as I could be.

I started by telling her that I didn't know exactly how it all worked. I explained that I might not know how to answer all her questions but I would try. Between you and me, I didn't even know if I knew all the appropriate terminology and I certainly would never want to offend anyone or put anything in Chloe's head that she might later offend anyone else.

So, we dived in.

I tried to explain to her that while people are born with *boy parts* or *girl parts*, they don't always feel—in their hearts—like they are a boy or a girl. She asked how someone *who was born with boy parts could grow boobs?* We talked about how transgender people—just like any people—are all different and everyone makes their own decisions for how they want their bodies to change, if at all, and that no matter what, we should always respect and love each other for whoever we are.

She was very engaged in the conversation and then she asked a question that revealed why she had been thinking about this to begin with, "Will I become a boy?"

Ah.

She went on to tell me that she had been nervous that she would *wake up one morning and be a boy*, and *is that how it works*?

I told her that she isn't going to just wake up randomly and BE a boy. I explained to her that it didn't work that way.

She wanted to confirm that she wouldn't just *grow a penis*, and then told me, with relief, "Okay, that's good, because I really like being a girl."

The conversation continued. I was interested to see how much she would say. We've always known Chloe is very introspective and always has a thousand things going on in her head, but it isn't often that she opens up and engages in a deep conversation, for more than a few minutes. Throughout our conversation, the rest of the table, with perhaps the exception of my mother, who was sitting across from me and quietly listening in (I think), kept their own conversations going. It never turned into a big table conversation.

She asked me if I knew any people who are *girls but used to have boy parts* or *boys but used to have girl parts*. I never, for even a moment, felt like she was being at all judgmental. She, like many of us, was just trying to learn as much as she could.

I asked her if she had any friends who had two moms or two dads. I wanted to bring the conversation to a level about acceptance and open-mindedness. I told her a story about a friend of mine who came out of the closet to his friends and family relatively late and asked her how difficult she thought it might have been to not feel ready or comfortable enough or safe enough to proudly be, to everyone else, who you knew you were for much longer. I told her that I believed it was our responsibility to always be accepting and to do everything we could to help make people feel comfortable and help give them a sense of belonging.

I asked her if it mattered to her if someone loved a man or a woman; if someone identified as a man or a woman, regardless of which parts they were born with. She said, "No, not at all."

I have always considered myself to be a pretty open-minded and accepting person AND I'm fully aware of the prejudices that exist and the difficulties people face. When any type of conversation like this happens with one of our daughters, I find that the hairs on the back of my neck stand up a bit and I get tense because my instinct is based on the context that I have about the world. This has happened before with similar conversations with the girls about the color of peoples' skin.

What became clear during this conversation with Chloe was that her context is very different—she seemed to inherently *believe* and *know* what many of us older people have had to *learn*: that being transgender or being homosexual aren't choices that people make, just like the color of someone's skin isn't a choice.

It just is.

Talking about these things and asking questions is how we learn and how we grow. It made me feel great—and proud— that her context is one of acceptance first.

She was only nine years old and was still teaching me something new every day.

CHAPTER TWENTY-THREE

*Sw*ar W!rds—Ages 8–10*

The girls have always loved music, and they learned when they were younger that song lyrics were available in apps like Apple Music and Spotify. Fun, right? Now, we can listen to whatever songs we want AND sing along. Secret bonus benefit—this was also a great way to practice reading . . . sort of.

Just take a moment and remember when you would sing along, with the most confidence, like this:

> It's gonna take a lot to get my Waze voice too . . .
> There's nothing that a million ten or more would
>   never do . . .
> I guess the rains down in Africa . . .
> Gonna take my time to do the things we never
>   made . . .

From "Africa(ish)" by Toto

Turns out I was singing the wrong lyrics forever. Before they had their own, the girls would just use either Danyael's or my phones and follow along with whatever song was playing. This is how I discovered an issue with Apple Music that may or may not have opened the door to a bit of a problem. As an example, I'll use the song "All About That Bass" by Meghan Trainor which was very popular for a time in our household.

After the following happened, I went back and looked it up in Apple Music. Was it marked as explicit? No way. Cool. Press play. Did I hear any swears? Not a chance.

Let's read along as Meghan sings:

> And all the right junk in all the right places
> I see the magazines working that Photoshop
> We know that SHIT ain't real
> Come on now, make it stop . . .

Julianna said, "Dad, why did she say *stuff* but the words say *shit*? What does *shit* mean?"

And that's where I believe it started (or it was some kid on the bus).

Danyael and I had a choice to make and we didn't know what other parents did in this case. There are different approaches we could take when it comes to *word management*.

We have always taken a *lean-in* type approach when it comes to any sort of conversation and we've done the best we could to stay consistent. We decided long ago that we would not shy away from any conversation that the girls wanted to talk about. Given how inquisitive kids can be, we wanted to always provide a safe place to ask questions and learn.

Now, we weren't and aren't some sort of bohemian or lawless household, not that there's anything wrong with that, where anything anyone wants to talk about is, by rule, always open. There are always exceptions. After all, there was that one time at the dinner table when one of the girls, and I can't remember which one because I think I blacked out, started the following exchange:

JULIANNA OR CHLOE: "Dad. Everyone has different bodies, right?"

ME: "Yes."

JULIANNA OR CHLOE: "So, like, people have different hair and different eyes and different skin colors and different sized boobs and different heights and different weights, right?"

ME: "Yes."

JULIANNA OR CHLOE: "Does that mean that penises can also be different sizes?"

ME: "Yes."

JULIANNA OR CHLOE: "So then, how big is your penis?"

Not many, but some, things are not great topics of conversation at the dinner table. This was one of them.

Back to the main story.

Julianna said, "What does *shit* mean?"

I've heard people talk about wanting their kids to take a sip of a beer with their parents. We all *know* our kids are likely going to try alcohol at some point. Why not do it within the confines of your home with supervision and then be able to discuss it?

We figured words could be the same thing. Let's just talk about how there are words that are not appropriate and we shouldn't use them but, the reality is that we will likely hear these words and we shouldn't be afraid of them.

We had rules. We told the girls that if they ever had questions about what a word meant or how it was used or why it was used or when it was used, they should just ask us. We talked to them about how other people—mostly grownups but maybe even kids in school—might use these words around them, but that didn't mean they were allowed to use them.

The internet, sex, puberty, swears. The *appropriateness semipermeable bubble* Danyael and I had worked so hard to keep Julianna and Chloe in, safe from reality, was rapidly expanding as they got older. That bubble would eventually burst, but we hoped it would not be until the time when they wanted to start building their own bubble for their own kids.

So, we started the conversation.

I said, "Shit can be a noun or a verb (#teachablemoment). It is another word for *poop* and works the same way. You need to poop or you just made a poop. See?"

There. We're finished, right?

Julianna said, "What does *fuck* mean?"

I suppose I'm glad she felt this comfortable. My hope was always that if we could establish a level of comfort with open conversations about (almost) anything (penis size notwithstanding), I knew when it would eventually come to the other big things (penis size notwithstanding), she and Chloe would both feel comfortable coming to talk to us. This is a good thing, right? Risk meets reward.

Here's one of those exceptions. I'm not going to explain the actual meaning of *fuck* to the girls. We are not there yet. Instead, I describe that it is an exclamatory word or an interjection; like this: "Oh, fuck!"

And so, we had our healthy conversation about these words and made the rules clear. They didn't use them outside the house (at least not when we were around) and they seemed to understand the power of these words and that they aren't necessary to communicate what they wanted to communicate. They understood that these words were not to be used with anyone other than us and it would really be better if they were not used at all. These words—like passwords to your computer or the code to the home security system—were not to be shared. They understood these types of words could even be funny sometimes.

When we were out in public and they would hear someone swear, they would give us a look of acknowledgment, maybe even smile, and then on with the show. They seemed to feel like they were in on the secret.

What I noticed shortly after this conversation, though, and found interesting, was MY reaction. It was likely unavoidable, while you're with your kids in public, that someone nearby might swear. It may or may not have been intentional. They may or may not know there were kids nearby. I've always found that most people try not to swear when they know kids are in close proximity. I also swear from time to time, but my years as a camp counselor and camp director trained me to choose the words that come out of my mouth very carefully. Of course, slip-ups happen.

When we were out in public and I would hear someone swear, or when we're watching a movie that we think is *safe* and some character swears, I used to jump in and [cough-cough] at the right time or try and distract the kids or do something to not draw attention—which in retrospect probably just drew more attention. Once those moments started happening, I knew the girls wouldn't be shocked.

I was confident that they knew words are powerful and meaningful. I also knew we would have many more words to discuss.

I don't blame Meghan Trainor or Apple Music for exposing my kids to swears. I don't blame other kids at school. I don't blame anyone. These words turned into another opportunity to teach our daughters a right way and a wrong way. They were going to hear them and learn about them at some point anyway.

We could have pretended the words didn't exist or even just said something like, "That is a bad word and you should never use it." A lot of people go that route and I neither judged nor disagreed with that type of approach.

I feel like Chloe and Julianna got it. Maybe I was wrong. Maybe we made the wrong choice. Who knows?

I sure as fuck don't.

Part V

Maturity

CHAPTER TWENTY-FOUR

The Talk—Ages 10–11

The following happened when Julianna was about to turn 11 and Chloe was about to turn 10. In the spreadsheet of a kid's life these days, it's pretty difficult to keep track of ALL the influences. You have:

- The internet (which we always did a pretty good job of monitoring/restricting)
- Bus rides to school
- Recess
- Dance class
- Summer camp
- TV shows and movies (that you don't always sit and watch)
- Many more

The reality is, no matter how good a relationship you have with your kids, no matter how good you feel about your level of communication, I suspect there is almost always more to the stories they know than they will ever tell. As a result, Danyael and I were cautiously waiting for the questions that are probably easy for THEM to ask and difficult for US to answer.

At the risk of sounding like the old man telling kids to "get off my lawn," I will say that it's difficult to see the social, retail, and entertainment aspects of society these days and NOT compare them to what it was like for me growing up. You walk through a mall and every clothes store, even the ones designed for pre-teens, have mannequins dressed like they're modeling for a Tinder profile picture. Even at the age of 11, Julianna had been asking for *belly shirts* for a few years.

Danyael and I had been very fortunate to have developed what I would classify as a really strong communication style with our daughters. As young girls, they generally did seem to ask us anything, no matter how awkward, and seemed to trust us enough to know they'd get truthful answers. This fact had contributed to my ever-growing sense that the talk about sex would be coming soon. There had been a number of occasions over the prior year or so when I've believed the conversation was on deck ranging from passing questions and comments like this one from Chloe:

> "Daddy, I don't want a baby. What do I have to do to make sure I don't have one?"

To this exchange with Julianna after, at an order-at-the-counter style restaurant, where we were assigned ticket number 59:

> (Julianna started giggling)
> What's so funny? (I said)
> 59 is 10 away from 69 (she giggled again)
> That's good math, but I don't understand why that's funny (I lied, uncomfortably)
> It's a sex number (she told me)
> I don't know what that means (I shit my pants)

Neither do I but I heard someone say it on the bus (I felt a moment of relief as I played dumb and realized I wouldn't have to explain this one . . . just yet)

And then a few days after that, Chloe asked Danyael, "How do babies get made?"

Semantically, this was a very different question than "Where do babies come from?"

The latter is the one we've had to answer before with things like, "from a mommy's belly." The former is much trickier.

Well, Danyael was able to punt until we could both be there (which we both believed would be a healthy way to have the conversation). We had some good fortune with our schedules to have a situation where Julianna was out at a friend's house having a sleepover so we had some quality one-kid time and figured it would be a good time to chat with Chloe so we waited for a nice, quiet time, and asked, "Chloe, Mommy mentioned that you had asked about how babies are made. Would you like to talk about that now, just the three of us?"

Danyael and I had done some research, read through some books, looked online, and spoken to other parents who have had *the conversation* already. We were ready.

Chloe answered, "No, I'm not ready to have the conversation just yet." Well, fine. How about that? Crisis averted, right? It's likely she just wanted to watch an episode of one of her TV shows but we weren't going to force the conversation. With that in mind, however, we knew that the toothpaste cap was off the tube and *the conversation* would be happening soon, just not that night and not with Chloe.

Skip ahead 24 hours and now, we have a bit more good fortune with the schedule because Chloe was out for the night and Julianna was alone with us. As you know, she's a year older and we figured, the girls talk so much, it was probably just as much on her mind as it was on Chloe's so we took a swing:

> "Julianna, we know it has come up in conversations, sort of, recently, and Mommy and I want to know if you are interested in learning about how babies are made?"
> She said: "I know how—sex."

And this is how the real conversation began. What follows is the way we chose to approach the topic. It might not be what's right for you, but it seemed like what was right for Julianna and for us. I hope you get a good laugh out of what happened next because it is funny, awkward, or both.

"What do you know about sex?"

She told us it was when two people kiss on the lips, "and like, make out," in a bed.

We agreed with her and that was the end of the conversation. Not.

We tell her that we're happy to have the conversation and that it is ok to giggle because it can be funny and awkward to talk about, but it is a serious topic and an important one. We also tell her that it is not her responsibility to tell her friends what she knows related to sex and that each parent decides when is the right time to talk to their kids is about it. So, if she has any questions, we're all ears, but that it really wasn't something to discuss with anyone but us.

She told us that she understood (and we believed her).

We started by explaining that a woman has ovaries—a part of the body that men don't have—and that ovaries produce an egg once a month. Now, for whatever reason, I was doing a lot of the explaining on this particular topic, so I may have gotten some of the biology wrong (I do not have ovaries). I explained that once a month, when a young girl is old enough, one of those eggs comes out of an ovary and lands itself in a protective *blanket-like* substance inside a woman's uterus (another organ I do not possess).

The egg just sits there—waiting—for some period (foreshadowing and pun intended) of time. This time is when a woman is *ovulating,* and is the time when a woman is most likely to get pregnant if she has sex. If she doesn't get pregnant, her body gets rid of the egg and the protective *blanket* and this is called . . .

Julianna jumps in, "A pyramid!"

Just kidding.

Julianna jumped in, "A period!"

We were on fire! This whole talk was going great (I remember thinking).

We continued. So, once a month, there's a new egg that is ready and if nothing else happens, it gets kicked out of the woman's body during her period. But, we explained, the egg is not enough. It needs something else to help it go from being an egg to eventually becoming a baby.

"What part do men have, that women don't have?" we asked.

"A penis!"

"Yes, and what else?"

"Balls!"

"Yes, and do you know the scientific/actual word for that?"

"Nuts!"

Exactly. Nailed it. It is worth noting that at this point in the conversation, I already was feeling a pretty strong sense of pride that Julianna was fully engaged with us.

So, we explained about testicles and how they produce something called sperm and that in order to make a baby, a single tiny sperm needs to meet up with the egg and you know, join together. Well, how does that happen?

We explain that while kissing on the lips, and *like, making out,* is a form of sexual activity, when people talk about *having sex,* they aren't really talking about that and they aren't really talking about how babies get made. What we wanted to talk about is something called *sexual intercourse*.

Here is where it got even more awkward (for you as the reader as well as for us as the parents at that moment).

She said, "Oh, is it this?" and then she started demonstrating something with her hands—you know the motion where you make the *okay* symbol with one hand and then you stick your other index finger through the hole, repeatedly? Yeah, that one (the one you are smiling about right now). She started doing that to show us that she *knew* what we were talking about. She was demonstrating this motion with a bit of a grin on her face.

I said, "Do you actually know what that means?"

She said, "no."

But she knew enough to know it was related to sex, right?

Well, I supposed we were going to have to explain.

"So, if we know that sperm starts inside the man's testicles and we know that the egg is waiting inside the woman's uterus, we just have to figure out how to get them together."

"A common way this happens is when a man's penis goes into a woman's vagina."

(I am having a difficult time even typing that.)

She giggled for a moment and then had a "Bruce Willis has been dead this whole time," moment (from the "Sixth Sense"), and then started laughing hysterically as she realized what that hand motion she was doing earlier really meant.

We all had a nice laugh at her realization.

We then went on to explain that once the penis is in the vagina, that's just not enough. The penis does something called *ejaculation* and a whole lot of sperm comes from the testicles and out the penis and essentially, start swimming up on a *treasure hunt* to find the egg.

We explained that there is one egg and millions of sperm and all it takes is one of them to find the egg and successfully get together and then, yada yada yada, 40 weeks later, a baby!

She seemed to understand the process and, in that moment, didn't have any real questions. We then took the opportunity to add in some *rules*. We explained that sexual intercourse was a very special thing to do with someone else and that it should only be done (in no particular order) when two people are old enough, care about each other a whole lot, know exactly what they are doing, and both REALLY agree to have sex with each other. We explained that it was a very special thing to share with someone and not something that should be shared lightly. We explained that the time it is right for one person might not be the same time that it is right for another person and we should always be respectful.

We also explained some of the other risks. We didn't want the conversation to be *over for good* or to be too heavy, so we decided to wrap it up. Danyael explained that as Julianna got older, when it was perhaps closer to the time when she might start to think about having sex, we could talk more specifically about ways to be safe and protected along with the other risks.

She nodded her head, seemed to still be relatively engaged, and hopefully learned a thing or two (I know I did).

I didn't know what would happen next.

As I alluded to earlier, one of our goals as parents has always been to maintain an open and honest relationship with our daughters so they always feel comfortable coming to speak with us about anything. The sex talk, while awkward at times, felt like it was really productive.

We decided we should and would check in more regularly to make sure if she had any questions, she had the opportunity to ask and could always get answers.

In the meantime, I figured I'd just be over in the corner, holding my breath and trying not to think about how my little girls perhaps weren't so little anymore . . . and hoping I didn't have to talk to them about the number 59.

CHAPTER TWENTY-FIVE

The Birthdays—The Future

I always enjoyed writing on my blog about my daughters on their birthdays. I did it for many years and almost every time, it was a bit of a *year in review*. As a little bit of an inside wink, these blog posts always were published at the minute that each of the girls was born. The reader would likely never know that, or pick up on it but it was something that I liked to do as a symbol of my appreciation for each of them.

Over the years I wrote many of these types of posts, but there was one for each that I enjoyed writing more than the rest: The one I told myself was a *crystal ball* post. The idea was to write a fictional story of how I thought Julianna and Chloe's stories might go. Here, for your reading pleasure, are those posts.

Julianna

2026

We are taking Julianna to Wellesley College for her freshman year (it is a great school, she has already expressed an interest in going there so she can be close to home, and I'm not complaining). She's a dual major and is studying early education and psychology. She told us in 2025 that she wanted to be a teacher, but between Danyael, you, and me, I think she'll end up being a guidance counselor.

She's always loved helping people and on a scale of 1 to 10 for empathy, she's an 11.

2030

She graduates at the middle-top of her class. She's fine. She works hard and does well, but I wouldn't say that she's passionate about school like her nerdy dad. During college, she had two boyfriends. She met the first one at a mixer with Brandeis University. He was really nice but he never went to summer camp and that was a nonstarter for her. Even though she's not in a rush to have kids, this guy was a bit of a rebel and doesn't know if he ever wants kids. Whatever, he's a nice guy and we're sure he'll have a successful career as a stockbroker on Wall Street.

The other guy; now, he was cool. She met him, coincidentally, at a different mixer with Harvard. The funny thing is, he didn't even GO to Harvard. He went to Boston University but was hanging out with one of his camp friends and decided to tag along. You read that correctly, he's a camp guy. They got to talking, realized they were both camp people, and really made a strong connection that night. I don't know all the details, and I don't want to know, but he treats her really well and they get along great. Things were going great . . .

2033

. . . right up until she told us that they were going to move in together. It is 2033 after all. I guess it isn't exactly how I thought things would go, but it's fine. She thinks he's *the one* and Danyael and I agree (between us). Neither of them are in a rush to make it official. She's a teacher in a local elementary school and he's working for Fidelity in Boston.

It has been difficult to not have her at all the family holidays because she goes to celebrate with his family now and then. His family is great and all, but it's difficult to look around the table and not see her.

She seems really happy with everything going on in her life which is nice. In a somewhat shocking twist, they decide to get a puppy. I remind her of how she used to be terrified of dogs and how when she got a puppy when she was six, she had to be carried around the house because she was afraid the dog would lick her face off. They name the dog *Becky* after her favorite character from Full House . . . yikes . . . too soon? It was 14 years ago already.

Life was great for her . . .

2035

. . . and then HE called and told me he was planning on asking her to marry him and could he have my blessing? What is this, "Anatefka" (from "Fiddler on the Roof")? It turns out that chivalry is not dead. At first, I'm thinking, she's only 27 years old. Is she ready for marriage? I'm thinking, it's 2035 and she can do whatever she wants. She's strong and confident and has a great career (loving the teaching thing). He's working his way up the ladder, although he wishes he wasn't wearing a suit and tie to work every day.

So, I say, "Let me check with my wife." We give him our blessing.

He posts his proposal on Facestagram and she clicks, "Yes!"

Just kidding, even in 2035 that would be pretty tacky.

He proposes (I'll let them tell you that story) in August. She says yes.

The following 13 months of wedding planning are *fun*. I do what I'm told and spend a good portion of the time working on my wedding speech. I also feel a great amount of anxiety about the first dance that we'll do together at the wedding. I'm not a good dancer.

2036

Wedding day! Even though I just turned 59 last month, I still look great in a tuxedo. I see Julianna for the first time in her wedding dress with all the makeup and the hair and the flowers and it blows me away. Ever since she was a kid, I've always thought that she was beautiful, both on the inside and outside, but there's something about seeing your daughter in a wedding dress . . . I'm not crying; you're crying.

The wedding is wonderful. Our first dance is awkward. My speech is hilarious. I make a joke about how I'm sure that everything she knows about sex, she learned from the talk we had back when she was just about to turn 11. It gets laughter from the crowd, a very red face from him, and Julianna covering her face with both hands. It's almost like she never learned that I've made it a life goal to embarrass her at the best (worst) possible times.

2040

"Dad, I'm pregnant."

My 32-year-old first-born daughter is going to have a baby. I'm not crying; you're crying. There's no doubt that she's going to be an incredible mother. We've always known that.

I can't believe that I'm 63 years old at this point and going to have another grandchild (more on the *another* later).

She has the happiest, most comfortable pregnancy. It annoys people all around her that she's so happy all the time with being pregnant. She gives birth to a beautiful baby . . .

Chloe

2027

We just got off the plane in Los Angeles. Chloe is about to start her freshman year at UCLA. I know what you're thinking because I'm thinking the same thing: There's no way she was going to choose a college so far away but UCLA does have a bear for a mascot, so. . . .

She does not have a declared major just yet, but she has been leaning toward getting a degree in economics while dabbling with their Computer Science/Video Game Design program. I know what you're thinking here as well—that I'm projecting. Unfortunately, in 2022, when it was year nine (I think) of COVID, she surpassed me in video game prowess. That was the first time she asked for a *video game rig* for her birthday (I was so proud).

2032

It turns out that Chloe decided to stay an extra year and get her master's degree in business administration. Before she graduated at the top of her class, she spent time working for the Daily Bruin and honing her writing skills. She really is well-rounded when it comes to school. While she is now far better than I am at video games, she's not quite as good a software engineer as I am . . . yet. That being said, she is strong in the ways of the force and for my 56th birthday, she built the app for me that I've been talking about doing (but not having the time) since 2015: What Have I Eaten (I'll explain some other time). She tells us she's having fun at school but is pretty opaque when it comes to details. We have no idea if she's been in any serious relationships. She won't tell us and she hasn't told Julianna. She did post a video on Instagram once with a guy but his face was clearly replaced with a Noah Kahan deep fake, so I'm not really sure what to make of it.

Continuing the trend of surprises, she decided that after she graduated, she would take a year off and travel the world.

2033

We are really happy that Chloe has moved back to the Boston area to a room down the hall from the bedroom Danyael and I share. She is starting her own software company (which I can't get into here just in case someone reads this and goes back in time to steal the idea), so we told her she can live with us while she gets the business up on its feet.

Danyael and I think she's in a relationship with someone because she's always on a call or FaceTiming with this guy. At first, I thought it was related to her company because they were talking about nerdy software things, but then we started hearing her laughing (in the non-nerdy way) about other things. Whoever this mystery person is, she seems to enjoy his company. With her, it's like pulling teeth, so who knows?

It turns out that the puppy Julianna and her boyfriend rescued had a sibling and Chloe asked us if it was ok if she could rescue that one because, she said, "We should keep those puppies as a family, even if they aren't living together." Obviously, we said yes.

Chloe is working really hard on her business. It's in *stealth mode* so there's very limited information about what's happening. I hear her clacking away on the keyboard and chatting with people in Meta Teams Collaborative Slack. There are a number of people on the team now and by the end of the year she has secured funding.

2035

It's September, I just turned 58 last month and to be honest, I'm pretty distracted by the wedding planning for Julianna. Chloe has since moved into her own place in Boston (at least we think so, because we haven't been invited over yet). Her company is doing well and they've released their game. I can't wait for you to get to play it. It's not surprising that she's the boss. Chloe comes over to have dinner with us and you won't believe what happens next (click bate): she says, "Mom. Dad. I have to tell you some news."

(Time slows down and I look to the camera for some exposition.)

Okay. Chloe was born in 2009. She is 26 years old and we've been waiting for the "I have to tell you some news" for a long time. Danyael is convinced she's going to tell us she's pregnant. But wait, that doesn't make much sense because she's drinking a glass of wine (but then again, one glass of wine isn't that bad). I'm pretty sure she's about to tell us that she got arrested. Nah, it's probably not that. She's always been so afraid of breaking rules . . . what could it be?

(Time speeds up.)

"I'm engaged."

I'm like, "Um, what?"

With a giant smile she says, "to [name redacted], of course. We've been dating for two years, you know, since I started the company." She is so happy.

I'm like, "Um, what?" The biggest surprise there is that I actually do know who [name redacted] is and I must be honest, I did not see that coming. Just wait until you find out who it is. #spoileralert

(We regroup.)

I have to say, I'm pretty excited (and relieved) for her. We always knew, unlike Julianna, that she wouldn't be filling us in on all the details along the way. It really shouldn't be surprising. The first person I ever *brought home* to my family was Danyael. They have no set timeline for when to get married yet. She explains to us that they make each other happy. We already know his parents and they are good people. She also explains that she wanted to tell us now because she didn't want to keep it a secret from us but wanted to make sure that Julianna and her wedding got the attention. This is oddly sweet of her.

2039

Julianna's wedding was incredible. I can't believe it was three years ago already. It took a while, but Chloe and her fiancé finally set a date of March 26th, 2039. This shouldn't surprise you. It's a few days after Julianna's birthday. Chloe has been waiting 30 years to appropriate that time of year as her own. It's the Park Place to Julianna's Boardwalk of calendar dates. The wedding is quite a bit different from Julianna's and just as special. After Chloe saw how awkward the first dance with Julianna was a few years ago, she finally relented to fulfilling my lifelong dream of a choreographed flashmob style dance. That was the trade she made for me promising not to mention the infamous sex talk I brought up during Julianna's speech. I have to be honest; I crushed the dance (not bad for a 62-year-old).

2040

You are NOT going to believe this.

"Dad, I'm pregnant."

I can't believe it, although I shouldn't be surprised. I always suspected Chloe would get pregnant before Julianna. They didn't waste any time. I can't believe I'm getting my first grandchild.

A few months into her pregnancy we find out that Julianna is also expecting her first child. This is so crazy. I'm so happy that they get to go through this experience together.

I didn't think this was possible, but her husband is now officially sick of eating mac and cheese, which was Chloe's #1 pregnancy craving. Chloe's pregnancy is a healthy one but I wouldn't say she was the happiest pregnant woman or the most comfortable. It probably didn't help that her sister was so cheery the whole time. Chloe keeps telling us that Julianna should, "just wait until she's another month along; she'll be miserable too."

After what seems like the gestation period of an elephant (up to 22 months), Chloe gives birth to a healthy baby . . .

CHAPTER TWENTY-SIX

Zen and the Art of Childhood Maintenance—Age 12

Julianna and I occasionally, to this day, go on a date night. I have done the same thing with Chloe.

One night when Julianna was almost 13, Danyael had arranged plans for her and Chloe to go hang out with one of Chloe's friends and her mother so Julianna and I did our own thing. She picked the restaurant (which happened to be my favorite local Italian place) and off we went. We arrived, got our table, and proceeded to have one of the deepest, most thoughtful, and most interesting conversations we've ever had.

We talked about insecurities. We talked about looking in the mirror and loving what we saw. We talked about anxiety and friendship. We talked about empathy and judgment. We talked about cakes of the lava and cheese varieties.

When writing, I have always tried to stay on the right side of Chloe's and Julianna's privacy. I've always asked myself, "If they read this paragraph in 10 years, will they be embarrassed?" As long as the answer is a reasonable "no," then I have kept it in. In the course of the conversation that Julianna and I had, we both shared things that we're insecure about and for her privacy, I'm not going to share some of those things here, just so you know.

The conversation started when we were talking about puberty and, in general, how everyone's bodies change when they go through it. At the time, she was at the beginning stages of change and had given Danyael and me lots of clues pointing at things she wasn't comfortable with. At dinner, we talked about a few of those things and I told her this . . .

"My hope is that one day, when you look in the mirror, you will see the beautiful person who I see in front of me."

She told me that while that was a sweet thing for me to say, that because I am her father, I was required to say that.

I told her that I was not required to say it, but even if I was, it was true in her case, anyway.

I tried to explain to her my philosophy on worrying and anxiety. There are certain things in life that we can control: How hard we work at math, what style our hair is, what kind of nutrition we put in our bodies, if we treat our friends with respect, etc. I then went on to explain that there are lots of things in life we can't control: How tall we are, when and how her boobs grow, when she gets her period, how our friends treat us, if the New England Patriots win, etc.

For me, I try not to sweat the stuff on which I have no control. Unfortunately, this is not always possible. We both agreed that while it would be nice to go back in time and have the chance to correct past mistakes or try something again with the knowledge and confidence we've gained since, that isn't possible. We could only move forward, control the things we can, and do the best we can with the rest.

Our conversation brought us to a discussion about empathy, which is something Julianna has in Costco-sized proportions. Julianna brought up her relationship with Chloe and this is when things got pretty interesting.

We ordered our meals.

Like most siblings—and particularly those siblings who are close in age—Julianna and Chloe have lots of ups and downs. As I've mentioned before, Julianna is emotionally like a dog in that she demonstrates unconditional love and wears her emotions on her sleeve. On the other hand, Chloe is emotionally like a cat, requires a lot of work, and might rub up against your leg incessantly or shit on your pillow to spite you.

Julianna is very secure and confident in her friend-making skills. When she has had issues with friends who might not treat her well, she pivots effortlessly. She knows the value of good friendships and has always been great at cultivating them. She is the go-to for her friends when they need advice. She's reliable and emotionally available.

At the time of this conversation, Chloe was not confident in her friend-making skills. She has since improved in this skill quite a bit but at the time, she was the opposite. She dealt with a lot of anxiety—which she couldn't really articulate yet—about her friends. When Chloe had issues with her friends, it was a much bigger problem. She put her eggs in a much smaller basket and hovered around that basket, trying to protect it because she was afraid of losing those friends. She always had been anxious about trying new things and meeting new people. I believe she was afraid to fail; that if she branched out, opened up, and made herself emotionally available, it would not be reciprocated.

The main course arrived.

Chloe did, and still does, have a nice inner circle of friends. We regularly encouraged her to focus on the positive relationships and we worked on spending more time with more (and new) people—to branch out. That same week, for the first time in as long as I could remember, she actively sought out plans with a new friend after school whom she hadn't hung out with before. She and this friend walked home to the friend's house after school. When she came home that night, it was clear that she had enjoyed a great day and was also proud of expanding her horizons. Baby steps. . . .

For Chloe, the comfort of what she knew, even if the situation wasn't always ideal, had typically outweighed the risk associated with branching out and potentially failing.

I could relate. I was the same way, and it was difficult to watch her struggle through it.

Julianna said, "If she would just open up and talk to me, I could help her. I'm really good at making friends."

I said that I agreed, but that perhaps we had to use that empathy, see the world through Chloe's eyes, and try to figure out the kind of help that she NEEDS to get, not the kind of help that we WANT to give.

Chloe's emotional availability was an issue that was difficult to relate to for Julianna.

Julianna said, "I just wish she would tell me 'I love you' more often."

She just wanted to hear more *I-love-yous*.

I told her about a philosophy class I took 25 years earlier in college. The professor (Dr. Lawrence Thomas) came in one day and posed a question to the class that I now posed to Julianna. I explained that there is no wrong answer and there is no right answer—but that I found it interesting to discuss.

"Do your parents love you?"

"Yes."

"How do you know?"

She took a moment and then started to list things. We told her every day. We provided a house, food, and activities. We gave her a sister. We helped with homework and gave her advice. We went on date nights and always had interesting conversations.

I asked what would happen if she asked all of her friends the same question. I asked if she thought they would all give the same answer—like they would if I had asked what 2 + 2 equaled. She said no, they'd probably give different answers.

I asked her how it could be possible that one seemingly black or white question would likely get different answers that are all correct relative to the person answering.

We weren't sure.

I asked her if she thought Chloe loved her even if she didn't say it, keeping in mind that Chloe might have a different way of expressing love than she did.

We talked about the fact that while Julianna and I agreed that hearing someone say "I love you" might be how we both *feel* that love, it might not be the way Chloe does.

We talked about some of the other things that Chloe does that might be her way of expressing love. Maybe her love is on display when she sits down on the couch next to Julianna and gently cuddles or maybe the way Chloe gets nervous when Julianna isn't on the bus with her on the way to school.

We all express our love and emotions differently.

"But why can't she just say she loves me without me having to ask? It would be so easy."

I said, "But why can't you just go to the movies [Julianna never liked going to the movie theater]? It would be so easy."

Empathy.

Who knows what the answer really was? I suggested to her that the next time she felt like she was not feeling the love in the way she'd like, maybe she should pause for a moment and try to see Chloe's perspective and understand that she simply doesn't express herself in the same way. It didn't mean the love wasn't there because someone else's love—just like how tall we are, when and how her boobs would grow, when she gets her period, how our friends treat us, and whether or not the New England Patriots win—are all things WE can't control.

Dessert time.

"But Dad, what is your answer?"

"To what?"

"How do you know if your parents love you?"

There are certainly things I know: $2 + 2 = 4$. There are other things I don't know ...

"All I can tell you is this; I won't speak for other parents but I can tell you my one goal: that you and your sister become happy people."

"Your happiness, in life, will be how you know I love you, and now ... leave me alone, I have a lava cake to eat."

CHAPTER TWENTY-SEVEN

Healthier Choices—Ages 44–46

In the winter of 2021, my dad had a bit of a health scare; a little more than a bit actually. He recovered, which is great. What's also great is that ultimately, it became a catalyst and motivational moment for me; I just didn't know it yet.

Let me give you a little background about ME—physically. I am 46 years old as I write this. For the first 40-something years of my life, I had a pretty skinny build. As a kid, up until my senior year of high school, I was also a really short kid. I'm fairly certain I was the shortest kid entering 12th grade. In that senior year, I grew close to a foot. I am now 6-foot-1 and no longer considered the shortest kid in the grade. *Sidebar*: Growing that much in such a short period of time is not ideal and I wouldn't recommend it. It has caused quite a few problems for my joints.

Also worth noting, I was always into sports. I know, I know; I'm a software engineer by trade and you don't think it's possible that I could also be good at playing sports, but the fact is, this guy right here was not only a really good basketball player and a varsity tennis player for years, but also a Little League all-star center fielder. I know what you're thinking, when I played Little League, I was really short and, therefore, nearly impossible to strike out. You are correct. I batted second and while not a power hitter, I was an outstanding table-setter with a remarkably high OBP (on-base percentage, for you nonbaseball nerds).

Other than sports, I didn't do much formal exercise, but because I played a lot of sports I GOT a lot of exercise. I was always in relatively good shape as a result. You combine all that with being what people would regularly remind me was *skinny* along with a fast metabolism and you get the ability to eat just about whatever you want, whenever you want. And I did. *Sidebar*: why is it that if I call you "fat," I'll get canceled but if you call me "skinny," it's totally okay?

As an example, not only did I *play* a lot of sports, I *watched* a lot of sports; particularly my dad playing in a men's basketball league. When he wasn't playing basketball, he played softball, and I'd go to those games too. This happened multiple nights a week. Without fail, after the games, basketball or softball, we would always go to a local fried food restaurant (Giovanni's or Land 'n Sea). I would always order a box of chicken fingers and fries and wash it down with a Coca Cola (the classic variety). Mostly, this *snack* would occur sometime between 9 and 10 at night.

I loved it.

This pattern of eating followed me into my 40s without any real issues. As an adult, if I had some sort of night meeting to go to (I'm involved in my town's government), I would go to Wendy's after the meeting and get two cheeseburgers and fries along with a Coke. This was my lifestyle.

Cholesterol you ask? It was always a tiny bit elevated, but never really a problem. I had my annual physicals that included blood work and it was never an issue . . . until it was.

In July of 2021, just months after my dad had his health scare, I had my annual physical. I was about to turn 44 at the time.

Given the *skinny* thing, I was never been considered as being overweight for my height, but also, I have never been a particularly good eater—as you might be able to tell. A few years ago, I learned that I was a supertaster (more taste buds, so my sense of taste is far greater than the average person). I have never liked the taste of alcohol, never smoked, despise broccoli, rarely eat (or even look at) green vegetables, can't drink hot liquids, and exhibit a variety of other food-related things that most people, including me, would consider weird.

But I do like burgers; I ate lots of burgers. I also like drinking Coke—a lot of Coke.

This was never a problem before, and while things like my cholesterol were never wonderful, it was never a red flag when I'd have blood work done.

Not until that day in July of 2021.

That day, my blood work showed that my cholesterol score was 247. It is worth noting that I'm not a doctor but I am an engineer, so the next part made it easy to understand for me. The optimal range we were looking for on the cholesterol number is between 140 and 200.

My Cardiac Risk score was 6.9 and the optimal range is between 0 and 5. If you read about supertasters, you'll see that there's a common pattern of higher heart disease risk for those people because of their lousy food choices.

My HDL (the good cholesterol) score was 36 and the optimal score is anything over 40.

Triglycerides you ask? The optimal range is lower than 150. My score? 1036.

Yes, you read that right: *one thousand and thirty-six.*

Maybe that was a false positive. Maybe not. All that information—along with my dad's health situation—was enough to catapult me into action. I was 0 for 4 on the cholesterol scoreboard.

My doctor, who is actually a nurse practitioner, called me that afternoon after the blood work came in to discuss options. I know what you're thinking: medication.

Nope.

She told me we should try some lifestyle changes before we start any medication, and that she had confidence in my ability to follow through. So many people in her profession would just immediately go to prescribing medicine. She didn't, and in my book (this book), that makes her the best doctor/nurse practitioner on the planet. It was time for change, Peter Brady style, so I needed to rearrange. I started that day.

She suggested I try intermittent fasting. She recommended I only eat between noon and 8 p.m., which gives your body 16 hours of fasting time. Something happens after a certain period of time where your body starts to eat its own internal fat (the part that gunks up the works)—and this can reduce cholesterol. She said I should do that four or five days a week.

I heard her recommendation of 4 or 5 days a week and raised it to 7 days because I'm a software engineer who likes routines and deals with lots of obsessive-compulsive tendencies. So that would be easier for me. She said, "Great, but if you get hungry, just drink water to fill your stomach up." Deal. "Make sure you still eat the things you enjoy [like chocolate lava cake]." Double deal.

Not drinking alcohol is a big component of intermittent fasting but since I already didn't do that, I was off to a good start.

I went cold turkey on my Coke situation. I have not had a Coke since that day in July of 2021.

We talked about cutting back on red meat. I have not had a Double Quarter Pounder from McDonald's (or a cheeseburger from Wendy's) since (before) that day in July of 2021.

We also talked about adding regular exercise to my routine.

As I got older, I'd slowed down a bit on playing sports. My ankles aren't great (thanks to the rapid growth spurt in high school), I have back problems, the IHOP early bird starts at 4, my mah-jongg card is out of date, and I have to get to bingo to meet up with Blanche, Dorothy, Rose, and Sophia.

But, okay. Let's rethink fitness as someone in their 40s. I started light exercise: running around my neighborhood, getting a few small home gym types of things, and trying to come up with some sort of regular schedule.

I also started to add protein shakes to my diet, including shakes that have *green* stuff that I hide in them. It would be better if I was eating the actual whole foods but having the powder supplements was better than the nothing I was eating before. I started trying to have healthier snacks in between meals.

After a few days of intermittent fasting, my body had adjusted to the schedule. I was not getting hungry until around noon. Gone were the late-night snacks.

Two months of this routine and I went back in for more blood work.

The cholesterol score was down from 247 to 201—not where it needed to be yet, but good progress.

The cardiac risk number was down to 5.6 from 6.9.

HDL? Stayed at 36.

Triglycerides: down to 282 from 1,036. Obviously, this was significant progress, but not near the sub-150 that we wanted.

I lost around 25 pounds. The goal wasn't to lose weight, but was a pretty drastic side effect of this process.

Onward we go.

It was hard, by this point, not to explain to my daughters why I was eating differently. I tried to do the shakes for snacks and lunch and make sure I could have a normal dinner with the family. They were seeing the changes to my routine and to my body and I wanted to make sure they knew the real reason why I was doing all this. I explained that I wanted to do everything I could to be around for as long as possible and that this whole thing was about having a healthy heart. This isn't about weight loss or happiness with my body or anything like that. This was about making healthier food choices and healthier exercise choices. It is worth noting that Julianna has what one might consider an unusual love for eating broccoli and Chloe has an equally unusual love for eating avocados. While they both enjoy sweets and less-desirable food from time to time, they are both actually pretty healthy eaters.

I'm an analytical person. I like to see proof that an experiment is working. I started to see small changes in my body before that second blood work, but when those results came back and there was scientific proof of progress, it became motivation to push even more. Exercise started becoming a really fun and import-ant part of my day—not just a chore. I started trying to figure out ways to do some sort of exercise or moving around every day. This was, of course, during the pandemic so my gym mem-bership (which I had, but was barely using) was useless.

The home gym started to evolve. We added a Peloton Bike, then a couple of weights, and a TRX suspension set (resistance bodyweight training). Eventually, we added a treadmill, a weight bench, barbell, more weights, and via an outstanding deal from a friend, a Hydrow (a rowing machine).

I don't want to say exercise and fitness, in general, has become an obsession—but that's just because I don't want to admit it. I love it. This isn't revolutionary, but when I exercise in the morn-ing, my energy for the day is so much better. As time went on, I was going every three months to get blood work and the num-bers were all trending in the right direction.

Keep going.

Jump ahead to April of 2023. I saw that a friend was changing careers to pursue a career in personal training because fitness always had been a passion for her. I sent a congratulations and, maybe joking just a bit, sent a message: "When are you going to put me on a plan?" You see, I'd been working out regularly but really just doing my own thing—what felt good to me. While it was working, I was always nervous I would do too much, hurt myself, or not do the right things. I figured if someone who knows what they are doing puts me on a routine, everything will be more efficient, progress will be faster, and I'll be able to do this work feeling more confident that I'm not going to hurt myself.

She started working with me that month. She would come to my house once a week with routines that I could do in my own home gym, and it was awesome. My confidence grew right alongside my fitness. Over almost three months, she gave me six different workout routines and helped make sure my form was right along with a schedule of when to work out. During the summer, I'm on my own because the schedule is a bit less consistent, but we'll reconvene later.

Eventually, July of 2023 rolled around and on the exact same day of the month, two years after I had my health awakening, I had my annual physical.

My cholesterol score, which two years ago had been 247, with an optimal range of between 140 and 200, was now 182.

Cardiac risk? That went from 6.9 two years ago down to 3.3, which is well within the 0 and 5 optimal range.

HDL (the good cholesterol) was at 36 originally, aiming for over 40, and was now 56.

Triglycerides? Two years before they were at 1,036 and were now 154: right on the edge of optimal. More work to do, but so far, so good.

Writing about myself in this way was never something I've been terribly comfortable with, but is something I think is important to share. After watching what my father went through with his health and then getting my own scare, albeit at a different level of severity, was a good, old-fashioned kick in the ass. While there are no guarantees in life and even for me, someone with all those obsessive-compulsive tendencies—there are only so many things I can control. I decided in July of 2021 that I would do everything I could to make sure that Julianna and Chloe had their father around as long as possible; even if they eventually get to a point where they don't want to hang out with me anymore (it's fast-approaching).

There are a lot of things in my life I'm proud of, with the top of that list being the father of two amazing daughters. I'm working hard to be a healthier person because there are too many things in the future that I don't want to miss. I am fully aware that there are people—maybe even you—who struggle with things that are far more serious, but for this moment, just this one moment, I decided to celebrate the progress I'd made. That's my choice for me and I think it's a healthy one. Every now and then, I hope you look in the mirror and see something about yourself that makes you proud. That's a healthy choice, too. Soon, it will be time to get back to work.

But first . . . leave me alone, I have a lava cake to eat.

CHAPTER TWENTY-EIGHT

Teenager Transition—Ages 13–15

I've found that each stage of my daughters' lives has brought interesting learnings, challenges, and a lot of fun. Throughout this book, I have tried to choose moments from various ages to illustrate some of those learnings, some of those challenges, and some of the fun. Like the previous *stages* of life, the teenage years—which we are currently experiencing—bring their own set of challenges. For me, as I write this, it's a challenge to talk about the girls' experiences without violating their privacy and without risking too much embarrassment. If you've ever met a teenage girl, you're a parent, or heaven forbid, a *dad*, you know that almost everything you say and definitely everything you do is *cringey* and brings with it a high risk of embarrassment, eye rolls, and a selection or combination of OMG, FML, and SMH. I figured I would start this chapter with the Jewish *gateway* to adulthood.

On Saturday, October 9, 2021, Julianna and Chloe had their joint B'Not Mitzvah. Because of how close they are in age, we decided that we would do their Bat Mitzvahs together. This worked out to be nice for both of them. Standing up in front of a large room of people and speaking is daunting for most people, and certainly when you're twelve and a half (Chloe) and thirteen and a half (Julianna). Doing it together was, I'm sure, a comfort for both of them. They worked incredibly hard practicing and preparing and, not surprisingly—at least to Danyael and me—were incredible. As part of their service, we wrote a blessing and then read it to them.

This is that blessing:

Chloe and Julianna,

Here we are, at the beginning of the Jewish year and at the beginning of the next chapter of your lives. Both of us are incredibly proud of both of you. You have both worked so hard for so long to prepare for this day. For months, we've had the pleasure of listening to muffled sounds of Torah portions and various prayer chanting coming through your bedroom doors. Today's accomplishment, like so many before, is the result of the hardest work you can do: sharing yourselves with your community; your true selves.

Chloe: We've always described you as being more like a cat. You tend to be a little shy at first. You enjoy quiet time and have always been introspective. You like to warm up to new people and new environments and approach both with caution. You get where you need to go when you're good and ready. You don't trust easily but when someone earns it, it's a bond for life. You have the best handwriting of anyone in our house. You have a very sharp and mischievous sense of humor. We've never met anyone who understood sarcasm as well as you did when you were a toddler.

Julianna: We've always described you as being more like a dog. You can't wait to see who is at the door. You want to be first in line to greet people. You show unconditional love for everyone you meet, right from the start. You love a good hug and will steal a chicken finger off dad's plate when you think he's not looking. Your sense of humor has always been a bit unintentional.

While you both share being sensitive, compassionate, smart, creative, and funny, you both do so in completely different ways and that's something that makes you so special and something that is so comforting for us, as parents. Even though you're so close in age, that you're similar in many ways and different in others shows that you're both on your own individual paths. You never walk one behind the other but rather side-by-side. Side-by-side into our respective offices during work because you are apparently oblivious to the fact that we're in a meeting.

Julianna, you were three months old when we found out that I was pregnant with another baby. We both had a moment of fear that we were taking your babyhood away from you. That fear was unfounded. It didn't take long for us to see how close you both would become and how necessary you both are for each other. I don't think you have any recollection of what life was like without having a sister. Seeing you both standing here together, leading together, and experiencing this together is a more incredible feeling than we could have possibly imagined. The bond that you share with each other is something that can never be broken. We know this because you both try—repeatedly.

Julianna, whether it was your first steps at camp, with Dan (a living legend at camp), or Chloe, your first time riding a horse, or either of your first times jumping in a pool, your first days going to kindergarten, your first time trying out for the volleyball team Julianna, your first time stepping up to the starting line and running in your first cross-country meet, Chloe, your first time reading from the Torah, or any of the first times in between, you've always managed to get the job done. Those times—like every future first in life—are likely to bring challenges, but your perseverance and your courage will continue to guide you through. You are both stronger and braver and more courageous than you recognize in yourselves— but we see it. We know it's in you. If you ever need a reminder of its presence, look to each other or look to anyone watching today. We all can use that reminder sometimes. Standing here today, leading this service, is further proof.

On your bedroom doors you each have a picture. One reads "Sisters by chance," and the other reads "Friends by choice." Dad and I are just lucky to have you as daughters. We are thankful that you both came along and completed our family. You teach us, every day, how to be better parents and how to be better people. Our best us is because of your best you.

For your whole life, I've been writing a blog about you both; about our experiences together—both the good and the bad—the things we've learned together, life, death, the challenges, and the triumphs. When I started writing it, I knew that someday you'd read it. I hope that day is soon.

We hope what you read there is a reflection of what you ideally see when you look in the mirror: Two beautiful people, both inside and out, on a life-long journey to constantly improve and to become great people: To be true to your unique selves and to change your worlds. To change your worlds, one friend at a time; one moment at a time; one hug or one smile or one joke or one kind act at a time. One goal at a time.

We see you. We all see you. The real you. And what we see fills us with pride and it fills us with joy. Every single day.

The B'Not Mitzvah was a wonderful event. The girls crushed their part and the party we threw was a hit. I'm not sure if you remember what was going on in the world around October of 2021 but as a reminder, I'll give you a hint: It started with C and ended with *OVID-19*. Because of this, we had all sorts of restrictions on how we could celebrate. For the party, we found an outdoor state park sort of place. It had a big open space where we set up a tented dance floor. It had two yurts: one for games and indoor things to do and one for a bar for the adults. If you've ever attended a Bar or Bat Mitzvah party, you know that most of them have themes. Finding a theme that worked for Chloe and Julianna was surprisingly easy: summer camp.

The food at Camp Brand was *camp-style* with grilled cheese, mac and cheese, and easy food like that. Even the adults liked it. Because of the time of year, we also had hot chocolate, s'mores, and even fried dough (the best part). We also were limited to having a total of 150 people (including the vendors) because of local COVID restrictions. The weather was perfect and the night got rave reviews (most importantly from Chloe and Julianna).

This day, for me, represents the beginning of the *Teenager Stage*.

I could mostly sum up this stage in one word: autonomy.

So much of this experience has been about seeking autonomy, figuring out what to do with received autonomy, and struggling with balancing autonomy. It's pretty tricky and sneaked up on us pretty quickly in this regard: When the girls were younger, they were pretty attached to us. They weren't super into being home alone or making their own plans or generally doing things without us. I guess this sort of independence is a bit of a slow boil. It has been my experience that neither Chloe nor Julianna ever articulated any sense of *I'll take it from here.*

Sort of all of a sudden, I turned into an Uber driver. I'm not sure there was a single weekend once the bar and bat mitzvah season started where I didn't drive a daughter somewhere and then somewhere back.

Julianna once asked, "Dad, can you take me to [friend 1's] house at 4:00, pick up [two friends], and take us to [third friend's] house so we can all get ready together before we go to the party?"

"Sure."

"Also, can you pick us up after the party?"

"Who is us?"

"You know: [friend 1], [friend 2], [friend 3], me, [friend 4], [friend 5], and [friend 6]."

"Umm . . . what time?"

"Well, the party ends at 10:30, so how about midnight?"

"That's confusing."

"Well, [friend 7] (who is hosting the party) wants us to stay after the party and hang out."

"Isn't the party itself the hang out?"

"Dad."

"I'm not getting you at midnight."

"Okay, fine. How about 11:45?"

"No. 11:30 and you must be ready to walk out the door. None of this 'we need 30 more minutes' once I get there."

"Kk." (This trend drives me nuts. I don't understand. If you're going to use two letters, why not use 'O' and 'K' as the language was designed?)

"Oh, one more thing, Dad."

"Yes?"

"We're all going back to [friend 1's] house for a sleepover after."

"So, wait, you're asking me to leave home, drive for 30 minutes to pick seven people up at 11:30 at night, and deliver ALL of you to someone else's house?"

"Yes."

And this sort of sums it up. Maybe I'm a sucker. I don't REALLY mind doing this sort of thing and don't want them to miss out on fun times, particularly when they are hanging out with friends.

So, to go back a bit, both Julianna and Chloe are now in high school.

In the year leading up to Julianna becoming a freshman, she regularly warned us of this impending independence and autonomy in the form of a self-nickname: High School Julianna.

- "High School Julianna is going to get to keep her phone in her bedroom at night."
- "High School Julianna is going to stay up as late as she wants."
- "High School Julianna will be sleeping until noon on weekends."

Parent Matt was mildly amused by this, sometimes.

Her sister though . . . not so much: "Middle School Chloe thinks you're annoying."

So, there we were: months away from the end of the middle school chapter of her life, high school just over the horizon, and another year of development behind us.

Earlier that calendar year, high school preparation started for Julianna in the form of her current teachers making recommendations about which honors classes she should enroll in for her freshman year. Before those recommendations, she told us that she really hoped—if no others—that her math teacher recommended her for honors math. When she was in the sixth grade, she had a math teacher who was, frankly, not good for her. Our fear was that she would be scared off from math as a result of this experience. She really struggled through math that year (I suppose it's a good thing I'm an engineer and a huge nerd who loves math—and no, I didn't do ALL her homework). Skip ahead and she was getting an *A* in math, was really enjoying it, and was hoping to get the honors recommendation.

I place quite a bit of the blame for her bad experience in sixth-grade math on her teacher that year and I give an equal amount of credit to her math teachers in seventh and eighth grades for her resurgence. We have been wildly lucky having incredible teachers for both Julianna and Chloe with that one exception.

The first recommendation she received was for honors English. This was also interesting, given that she really stopped enjoying reading when she was around 8 years old.

Honors civics. Honors science.

Who was this nerd now?

And finally: honors math. Julianna was so proud of herself, and rightly so. She had worked so hard and earned those recommendations.

When it came time to actually choose her high school classes (a student doesn't have to take the recommendations if they don't want), she chose to enroll in honors English and honors math.

You want to know the electives she signed up for? The first one was ceramics. Awesome. I couldn't wait for another ambiguous pencil holder/coin tray. If you knew Julianna, you might have a hard time understanding this second one: Human Behavior and Genocide.

We're talking about Julianna here; a person who still wouldn't watch "Frozen" because it makes her too sad (don't even get me started on "Frozen II"). I don't want to harp on all things school here, but this was actually a bigger deal than the specific class.

Julianna had a chance to take lots of different classes, and without consulting with us, she studied her options and decided that she was going to lean into something that made her really nervous and would be potentially very challenging. This is just not something she would have been willing to do in previous years. Epilogue: she ended up switching out of this class.

She was growing up. This makes sense given the theme of seeking and proving autonomy. She also volunteered to be a team manager for the middle school girls' basketball team (never played basketball). She would make her own plans and sometimes considered the fact that I really wasn't an Uber driver. She had learned how to cook and even better, she learned how to bake. She enjoys both of those things.

She was actively seeking out and finding more independence this year, faster than any of us expected, but still found time to call—or at the very least text—my in-laws and my parents to see how they were.

Julianna got her braces off at the beginning of this phase and started wearing contact lenses (sometimes/rarely). Her idea of teenage rebellion, for that time, was to not wear her lenses or put in her retainer at night. She's showing us who's the boss!

Through all the changing and growing, there were two things that remained constant: her empathy and sense of emotion.

At least for a little while, she would regularly interrupt whatever it was I was doing to just give me a hug. It would happen during Zoom meetings. It would happen when I'm walking down the hall. She was the master of the sneak-attack hug.

She never stopped being a great friend, a great sister, a great daughter, and a great person in general. High School Julianna was on the right track. I'm sure we will settle into that version of her just in time for College Julianna to launch.

This is also the phase of life when many people start to experiment, at least with the idea, of drinking alcohol. I'm not going to get into much of that here because it feels like it crosses the privacy line a bit. It is worth noting, however, that I HATE the taste of alcohol. It's just not something I've ever enjoyed and have never been a big drinker. I suspect at least one of my daughters might *suffer* the same fate. That being said, given the years of open and honest conversation about anything, our hope was that the girls would talk to us about this type of thing as well.

I'll sum up the alcohol topic here: Our hope turned into reality. We continue to have great conversations about alcohol, who is consuming it, where it happens, how it works, how to be safe, etc.

Given our style of communication, they tell us about this sort of thing all the time. If they are going to a social gathering of friends and believe there will be any drinking, they let us know, tell us if the parents will be there, who will be there, what kind of alcohol there will be, and if it's okay if they partake; how much they can partake. Danyael and I have this odd tightrope to walk: Do we want to *approve* of drinking alcohol and be part of the conversation, along with our advice and rules OR do we want to *disapprove* of drinking alcohol and risk being shut out and then just having them do it anyway?

We chose the former. They are teenagers and the reality is that they are absolutely going to be around alcohol. That is not uncommon for people their age (and older). I would rather they talk to us about it and give us the subtle chance to coach them on how to make smart decisions than not. When it comes to drinking, vaping, etc., many people their age are influenced—either passively or more directly—by their friends or what's happening around them. In our case, they certainly get a lot of that, but for the moment, also from us. Each time I go to pick one of them up from one of these gatherings, I get a rundown of what was going on. I appreciate this.

They are going to do what many teenagers do. I have no doubt about that. The only question is: Do I want to be part of the conversation or not?

This is all about making smart decisions.

The reality is, this is the stage that seems to require—for the first time—an equal amount of transition for the parents as it does for the kids. I have had to get used to having less control and less knowledge about what's happening in their lives. They will share what they want to share. All I can do is help make an environment where they feel safe and not judged, with the hope that they will continue to communicate, seek advice when they want it, and hear advice when they need it.

So how have I chosen to keep myself sane through all this? Embarrassment.

They already tell me how embarrassing I am, even if I do nothing. If that's going to be the case, I might as well lean in and *actually* be embarrassing. For example, there was this one night when Julianna was home studying for a high school quiz in her Health class; it was about female anatomy, and specifically, the vagina. At home, she told me all about what she was learning. How thrilling! I told her that when I dropped her off at school the next day (fortunately, it was my week to drive the neighborhood carpool), perhaps I would just yell out, as she was walking away, "GOOD LUCK ON YOUR VAGINA QUIZ!"

"Dad. I will never speak to you again."

Challenge. Accepted.

We pulled up to school, she looked at me. I looked back at her. The world slowed down. I could tell she was anticipating the worst. She was preparing to be embarrassed and I hadn't said anything yet. As she started to walk away, I said:

> "Good luck on your . . ."
> The blood drained from her face as I paused.
> ". . . quiz."
> She smiled.
> (relief).

And so, High School Julianna and High School Chloe walked toward the school knowing they may have escaped without a terribly embarrassing moment. They started to walk faster when I imagine they both thought the same thing: He was waiting for us to get more distance from the car and closer to other students before he swung for the fences.

I drove away, victorious.

CHAPTER TWENTY-NINE

Love and Learnings

I have lived a pretty incredible life so far.

I always knew I'd want to have kids someday but never really felt confident about how it would happen. Generally speaking, I was a pretty confident person when it came to things like academics, Legos, video games, and sports, but not when it came to relationships. I guess I had faith.

Way back in the book, I told a bit of my story but left out the part about how this whole parenting thing started.

My best friends and some of my funniest and best experiences come from Camp Tevya, which I began attending in the summer of 1988. Back then, you had a choice: you could go to camp for the first four weeks, the last four weeks, or the entire eight weeks. When I started in 1988, I went for a month. It was the first time I had ever been away from home for that long and the first time I had been away from my parents for more than a weekend. I never looked back. I was a camper until 1992, which was the summer I was about to enter my sophomore year in high school.

At camp, there is a tradition that still exists where the youngest campers and oldest campers choose what we call *Royalty*. The youngest boys choose a princess. The youngest girls choose a prince. The oldest girls choose a king and the oldest boys choose a queen. These selections are a surprise. The campers—for as long as I've known—march around the dining hall singing song parodies that are filled with clues, slowly hinting toward their choices. These selections have almost always been a camp counselor (I can think of one time when the choice for king was the head chef).

In 1992, it was my turn to be part of the group that chose a queen. Our counselors helped us choose who she would be. The person they recommended was not someone I knew, which made a lot of sense to me given that well . . . she was a girl. We worked on our songs and ultimately crowned our queen. It is safe to say that while I had a lot of friends and people liked me, I was probably not considered to be one of the *cool* people. She, on the other hand, was generally considered to be one of the *very cool* people. This might not be a huge surprise to you, but we didn't spend a lot of time talking to each other in 1992.

In the summer of 1993, she was back at camp, still as a counselor and I was there as a counselor-in-training. This paragraph can be really short because I think I spoke with her even less that summer than I did the summer before. Her name was—you guessed it—Danyael.

Skip ahead to the spring of 2005. There had been one time in the intervening years where I saw her at a concert in Boston (she's from New York). She emailed me to tell me that her dad, who had worked at the very same camp in the 1960s, would be returning to camp and be in charge of *Land Sports*. She knew that I was also returning to camp as the head counselor for all the male campers. She was not simply letting me know that he'd be there, but also asking if I would look out for him.

On July 1, 2005—a Friday—she and her mother came up to camp to visit her dad. Around 2:00 in the afternoon, I was walking back to my cabin, apparently shortly after they arrived. This was the first time she had been back at camp since 1993 and was going for a walk with her mother. We ran into each other at a place in camp called *The Crossroads*. This area, as you might imagine, is a spot where a few roads cross with a tree at the center. She introduced me to her mother and I volunteered to walk with them and show them around. This was my *queen* after all. Even though I was quite a bit older than the last time she had seen me there and SIGNIFICANTLY taller, I was still quite giddy.

Almost immediately, we came across a group of campers participating in a yoga class (this camp has a wide variety of activities). Her mother decided she wanted to participate, leaving just the two of us to continue the tour. We ended up spending the rest of the day together, and I'll be honest; it was a great time and since I've always been oblivious to relationship vibes, it was totally innocent and without any awkwardness (that I was aware of).

That night, which was a rainy one, it was my turn to deliver snacks to the counselors who were charged with covering the bunks while other counselors had free time. Because it was raining, I loaded the snacks into my car. She decided—I assumed because she was bored but perhaps in retrospect for other reasons—that she would come with me. The first moment I became aware that there might be some sort of spark going on was when she offered to arrange the snacks in order by cabin for efficiency. We had a lovely time driving around delivering snacks.

Eventually, all of that was done and my responsibilities for the night were finished. This was around 1 a.m. The rain had stopped and I walked her back to the place where she was staying (a temporary mobile home with one of my best camp friends who happened to also be a head counselor for the female camp-ers that summer). At this point, even I—with my poorly cali-brated social-cue radar—knew something was afoot. We walked down to an area of camp near where she was staying called *The Riviera*. This is a mostly grass area with a bunch of trees right on the edge of the lake, and this—*this spot*—is where we had our first kiss.

We started long-distance dating *officially* after the summer ended. We saw each other every other weekend. We would alternate visits, so once a month I would go to New York City where she lived and then the next time she would come to Bos-ton where I lived. It seemed pretty clear that we were aligned on how the relationship was going and what we both wanted. When I would go to NYC to visit, I would typically get on a bus called the LimoLiner on a Friday, around noon. This was the first type of bus that had Wi-Fi, so I could work during the ride.

On May 19, 2006—a Friday—I was on my way, just like most of the other visits. The difference this time was that in my right jeans pocket, I was carrying an engagement ring in a box. Of course, there was a ridiculous amount of traffic, and the ride—which normally took four hours—took closer to seven hours. My nerves were already through the roof from sitting in traffic and I could barely feel my ass from sitting that long. Add the pressure and uncertainty around an impending proposal, and it made for a pretty tense version of myself.

Once she knew that I was delayed, she told me that she would be at a restaurant near her office (where I'd normally go meet her) with a friend and that I should just come there when I arrived.

Swell.

Finally, the bus got to NYC. It had a drop-off at a Hilton hotel on 6th and 55th, so that's where I got off and started walking. Now, because I had a whole plan for how this proposal was going to happen (which would have been hours earlier), I had moved the ring box to my laptop bag. Trust me. I had a very specific plan in mind. I got to the restaurant and Danyael and her friend were sitting in a booth right next to the door. I was pretty spent with the whole traffic-delayed journey plus the anxiety around the proposal so I wanted to get out of there. Danyael, not knowing what was about to happen, encouraged me to sit down next to her and to just "throw your laptop bag on the booth seat next to [her friend]." This seat was within arm's length of the door, so I didn't want to put it there. It not only had my computer, but also the ring . . . and all I could think of was someone might snatch the bag and run off, ruining *everything*. This added to the anxiety that I assumed was radiating off me. I would later learn from her that my assumption was correct.

Finally, we made our way back to her apartment, which was in midtown near 56th and 8th. She lived on the 18th floor and had a beautiful and unobstructed view of New York City at night. The neighboring buildings were not that tall so you could see far. I deliberately placed my laptop bag on the floor (not on a chair or table).

She told me she had something for me. This was a wrinkle in the plan. It better not be an engagement ring, I thought. She told me it was small. She gave me a buff from the show "Survivor." This is a TV show we bonded over from the beginning and still watch to this day. This Survivor buff actually worked perfectly with my plan. I told her I had something small for her as well. First, I went into my laptop bag and pulled out a T-shirt from the software start-up where I was currently working. How thrilling!

I then told her I had one more thing, but it was even smaller. In order to get it out of the laptop bag, I had to get down on one knee. I knew she'd be suspicious if I just randomly got down on a knee, which is why I had this whole schtick about the one other small thing and made sure the laptop bag was on the floor. It was all so *natural*.

I took out the ring box, opened it up, and turned around on my knee. This is the moment when her hands went up and covered her mouth. I said what I said (just between us) and then asked her to marry me.

I then stared at her for what felt like hours of being stuck in bus traffic.

Eventually, I said, "So?"

She said "Yes."

I'm not making this part up: a moment later, we looked out the window of her apartment and saw fireworks going off. She asked if I planned it. There are a few odd things about this. No. I didn't plan that. Had I not been delayed because of traffic, I would have proposed hours earlier and we would likely never have seen the fireworks. Also, it was May 19 and we had no idea why there would be fireworks. It was not a holiday.

So that was May 19 of 2006. We got to work planning the wedding and got married on February 25 of 2007. We move fast.

Julianna was born in March of 2008. Chloe was born in April of 2009.

That is how I became a husband and a parent.

I take being a good husband and partner very seriously, but being a good parent has easily been the greatest and most rewarding journey of my life. There's not enough thanks I could give to my wife, Danyael, for making me a father.

I have prided myself on being as involved and engaged a parent as I could be. I have learned and loved more over the years of being a parent than I have learned or loved in any other period of my life.

Dear Julianna,

One of the first things that went through my head when I watched your birth was, "Oh wow, I'm a dad now." I'm not sure I can think of any person, or even a type of person, who was better suited to introduce me to the things it takes to be a parent. Your warmth, grace, empathy, sense of unintentional comedy, and willingness to always help far outweigh your instinct to sleep until noon and then sleep any other time of the day when you don't have school or friends to be with. Your willingness to go with the flow and to try new things has always been admirable. Your ability to properly navigate the peaks and valleys of friendships and communicate how you are feeling at any time is something I envy. The way you start crying, for no apparent reason, and then laugh through it because even you can't explain why it's happening is a skill I hope you never lose.

Dear Chloe,

When you were born, I had a whole year's worth of parenting confidence under my belt and much less in the way of nerves. From your very beginning, the intelligence you displayed and your ability to understand what was going on around you and to grasp new skills and concepts was something that I found incredible. I knew from very early on that I was watching someone grow who had so many of the same qualities that I see in myself. These are things that I've always considered to be my superpowers and I know they are yours as well. Your sense of humor, from the moment you could communicate in any way, was so far beyond your years that I sometimes wondered if I was being pranked. I've never met anyone who so quickly understood my sense of humor. Watching you figure things out and, in general, watching how your brain works has always been so exciting for me. Seeing you deal with a lot of the same anxieties that I dealt with when I was your age has been really difficult for me, but I've always taken solace in the fact that I figured out the tools I needed to be successful—and believe me when I say, "I see you improving every day." You may not notice as much as I do, but there are things that used to be mountain-sized problems for you that are now tiny hills. It is your resilience—and frankly, your stubbornness—that I think drives you toward improvement and I have been so happy to see you take steps forward every time. I believe you will change the world and I can't wait to watch it happen.

To both of you:

Being your father has been and is the greatest honor of my life. As someone who considers himself to be a person of science, I can't wrap my head around how illogical it seems that I have been so lucky to have two wildly different daughters who, together with Mom, have made for me the most perfect family.

I simply am not the person I am without you. You have made me better in all ways. I know it isn't always easy. I know there are times when I annoy you or embarrass you or maybe don't even live up to your expectations, but I can promise you that every day I wake up with a mission to be the best parent, the best friend, the best listener, the best advice-giver, the best hugger, the best husband, and the best dad that I can possibly be:

- I will never stop trying to improve
- I will never stop trying to help you
- I will never stop wanting you to be happy
- I will never stop being there for you in whatever way you need me
- I will never stop being proud of you
- You will always be the most important part of my life
- For all that has happened and all that will happen, thank you
- *Thank you* for being the best daughters a parent could ask for

I love you both.

On the next episode . . .

Mid-Credits Scene

Ever since I started writing this book, there have been a number of moments that triggered in me the desire to write. In the past, each of the moments COULD have turned into a blog post but in honoring the premise of this book and Chloe and Julianna's privacy, rather than writing, I just made mental notes in the hopes that I would find some way to write about these moments in some form, even if only at the highest of levels.

These days, many movies will show some sort of mid or post-credit scene that illustrates an epilogue of sorts—this is that.

What's been happening since I started writing this book:

- *Chloe only took about two days of going to high school to get into the groove.* Transitioning to becoming a high school student is obviously a huge deal and Chloe, who has not always been *wonderful* at transitions, took this one on like a champion. She is a straight-A student.
- *Part of what helped with that transition*: Chloe decided she wanted to try out for the Field Hockey team. She had never

played before but had some friends who had and they convinced her to try. This is also something that, up until this moment, she had never been incredibly open to: trying new things. Trying out for—and making—the freshman field hockey team (which started before the first day of school) gave Chloe a sense of belonging and comfort on this new phase of her journey. She's a sneaky good athlete (like her father) but hadn't shown a huge interest in competing prior to this year.

+ *Julianna got her learner's permit and we have been spending a lot of time driving.* I strongly dislike not being in the driver's seat in a car and so this was a huge challenge for ME to get over. I believe she will be a good driver but I haven't actively experienced shitting in my pants quite so frequently since I was a baby. She does a good job of talking out what she's doing while she's driving as if she is a contestant on "Who Wants To Be A Millionaire."

+ *Both Chloe and Julianna are on the high school tennis team.* They both enjoy playing tennis and they take lessons throughout the year. Julianna played on the team as a freshman and earned her varsity letter (one must play in at least one varsity match in order to do so) that year. That meant she didn't even need to try out as a sophomore. Chloe did have to try out, and made the team. Julianna played varsity the entire season. Chloe, like her sister, earned her varsity letter during the season as well. At the end of the season—after the team had been eliminated from the playoff tournament—there was one final practice and the parents were invited to participate. As a tennis player myself—and to be consistent with my mission of embarrassing my daughters—I was challenged to partner with Julianna's partner's mom (who also plays) and play against Julianna and her partner. I'm fairly certain they both thought they would crush us. While my partner and

I were invested in making this a fun experience, I think we both reveled in the idea that our respective daughters were underestimating our skills. She even texted me the night before: "Let's crush their spirits!" We played one set and beat them six games to four. Old people: 1—Young, cocky teenagers: 0.

• *Chloe geared up to go back to camp for her final summer as a camper.* This was hard for us all to believe. It's been quite a journey for her and she was REALLY excited. The final summer as a camper is very special and she'd been waiting a long time to get to participate in all the fun traditions. When going to camp was exactly one month away, she said, "Dad, camp is one month from today and so I will not be sleeping tonight." Julianna participated in a leadership program with camp that involved traveling to Spain and Portugal with not only her whole age group from camp but also the teens of the same age from the two sister camps. I was a counselor on this trip in 1998 and I know it is something she will never forget. This is the first time since 2021 during COVID that Chloe and Julianna won't be at camp together. It didn't go great that year but was much better this time, given how special the summer was for each of them. The good news: Julianna (and her entire age group) got to go back to camp for the final week and a half. Chloe—always reticent about well, everything—was secretly really excited to have her back.

• *I took Chloe to the doctor for her annual checkup after she turned 15.* This was the first time that I was afforded the opportunity to do so in four years. Don't get nervous. I was only in the room for the first few minutes while we discussed the year that was and then I went out to the lobby for the real exam. I loved doing those visits when the girls were younger but as they entered the teenage years, it felt like it made less sense for me to be there. This time Chloe was ok with me coming, which I think was perhaps some sort of gift to me. *Sidebar* (that might seem related but isn't): I heard a rumor that once you get your period, you're probably only going to grow around two more inches.

- *Me? I'm doing great.* I mean, I wrote this book and got it published. I am still a software engineer and love building products that make a difference for people. I continue to serve on my local School Board as an elected official. Ever since my health *issue* in 2021 I have gotten more and more into fitness and health in general. Danyael even surprised me and arranged to have our basement home gym turned into a finished space that rivals what you'd see in a professional gym—and it's become my favorite place in the house. My cholesterol is good, thank you very much.
- *Based on the previous rumor, I have not gotten my period yet.* Thus, I'm hopeful that I'm still growing—in height and as a person.

Special Thanks

When I started on this journey, I wasn't sure where it would go and I suppose that's part of the point. I didn't write this with any sort of delusion of grandeur that I would become a world-renowned author who gets his book made into a giant Holly-wood movie (although an indie film that plays at Sundance wouldn't be awful).

As I've gone through the process of writing, editing, and fig-uring out how book publishing works, I've learned a ton and had help from all sorts of people. Without them, this would all be in a vacuum. With that, I want to share a few special thanks to those who helped me get this book to where it is now (in no particular order):

- **Julianna and Chloe:** They are, of course, the inspiration for all of this. They've known for a long time that I was writing about them but they didn't find out about this book until after I finished the first draft. I sat with them at the kitchen table one night and revealed that this was happening. The first question, from Julianna, was, "Can you read us the last sentence?" When I said, "I love you both," Julianna started crying and then Chloe started welling up watching Julianna cry.

Over the course of working to get this published, people have asked me what my goals were. One of the biggest goals was to have an artifact, something my daughters could always have as a way to remember their childhood (at least from my perspective). I cannot thank them enough for being so supportive of all my shenanigans all these years. I promised them that I will keep trying to embarrass them for as long as I'm capable.

- **Danyael:** She's the person who gave *me* the confidence to be *me* a whole bunch of years ago. She, like Julianna and Chloe, didn't know I was writing this book until after the first draft was complete. Similar to our daughters, this wasn't possible without her support. We make a great parenting team (at least in my opinion) and for as long as I've been writing, has been the sounding board for everything I've written. She was the first person to read the first draft of the manuscript and she didn't even throw up all over the place after doing so.
- **Marcia:** My aunt spent time, in between the work that she actually gets paid for, doing an editing pass of the entire book. What everyone tells you when you sit down to write a book, and what you don't believe, is that you NEED someone other than yourself to edit the book. You become blind to typos, punctuation and grammatical errors, and countless other suggestions. Marcia spent a lot of time working to help me make this higher quality. She's also the aunt who would take me to Toys "R" Us (and later to Electronics Boutique) on my birthday when I was a kid and tell me to pick out whatever I wanted. These were

some of the most joyful moments of wonder and excitement for me as a kid.

* **My parents, sister, and Benjie:** This group of people read the manuscript and were totally unbiased in expressing their love of it. I'm a fairly confident person when it comes to *work* things but even so, having people you trust tell you that something you've done is enjoyable or relatable or good in any way feels good and is reassuring—even with the built-in bias—that I've not been wasting my time doing this.

* **Bobby and Steve:** You don't know each other but you've both given me so much helpful information about how the book publishing and marketing process works. I may never be Stephen King, Michael Crichton, Colleen Hoover, or Plato but your willingness to help me learn this process has been invaluable.

* **You:** I would have given you credit for reading this book even if you hadn't gotten this far. For anyone to take the time to read something that this no-name, first-time author has put together and hopefully find some amount of joy from doing so is quite an honor. I appreciate the time you've given to this book and hope you've laughed a little, maybe cried a little, and perhaps spent some time reflecting on your own experiences.

Epilogue

In the foreword, Chloe referenced a book she was working on when she was eight years old. It was called *New Girl*. What you are about to see is the result of that effort. Remember, she was eight years old when she typed this. Fortunately, she typed it in Google Drive and Danyael was able to find it all these years later. I left it untouched, aside from formatting. Warning: it is long and incomplete but I wanted to include it so you could experience the glory that is Chloe's mind at the mature age of eight. Now, for your reading pleasure, I give you *New Girl*.

New Girl

by Chloe (age eight when she wrote this)

Dear Diary,

New school, new friends, new teacher.

Story of my life! Once upon a time there was a girl named Emma. She was trying to make friends at her new school,

Kennedy Middle School. When she arrived at gym class two girls came up to her.

"Hi, i'm Olivia, and this is my best friend, Violet. What's your name?" asked Olivia.

"Ummm, hi, i'm Emma, the new girl. Nice meeting you."

"Wait," said Violet, "do you want to be a gym group with us?"

"Sure, I guess."

"Whew," they all said at one time as they ran out of the gym. "I did not know that gym could be so fun," said Emma panting. "Hey, do you guys want to come to my house after school so we can get to know each other better?" said Emma hopefully. "Sure," said Violet.

After school ended they scrambled to get out. When they arrived at Emma's house, her 2 younger siblings, Dustin was playing with legos and Tessy who was playing with dolls but was now running over to Emma to probably tell on her brother. "Hi Tessy!" shouted Emma. "This is my little sister Tessy, also known as my favorite sibling," Emma whispered. "We are going up to my room."

"Don't care!" scowled Dustin.

Emma frowned. Welcome to my world. As they were walking up the stairs Emma's mom was coming down the stairs. "Hi Emmy!" Mom said. "Hi Mom, Bye Mom."

"Slow down," said Mom, "let me meet you friends."

"This is Olivia and Violet."

"Good to know," Mom said quietly. "You may go now."

As they approached Emma's room a small golden retriever jumped off the bed. "This is Sandy. I got her when I moved here. So she is only 2 weeks old," said Emma. "I love her already," said Violet. "She's so adorable," said Olivia.

Incoming!

Just then Tessy ran in and took a big leap onto Emma's bed. "Hi!" Said Tessy dramatically. "Hey," said Emma.

"You wanna go for a ride?"

"For ice cream?"

"Yes! Yes! 1,000 times yes" screamed Violet. "Now we'll tell you. Follow me!" Said Tessy excitedly. "Where are you taking us?" Asked Olivia. "Here!" Said Emma. "A meadow?" Asked Violet. "Turn around silly," said Tessy.

"WHOA! You have a barn." Olivia screeched. "Let's go inside." Emma motioned. A chestnut colored horse's head appeared from inside a stall. "That's Belle," said Tessy. "You guys want to help tack up some of our best horses?" "Duh!" Exclaimed Violet. "I am on Belle. Tessy you are on Captain. Violet you are on Steel. Olivia you are on Secret." As the girls were just about to mount the horses a big black van pulled up in front of Emma's house. A boy with brown hair jumped out of the van.

"OH! That's my brother, Zach. So I bet it's time for me to leave. Bye!" Said Olivia as she hustled down the big meadow to the van and hopped in. The van pulled out of the driveway. "Now that Olivia left do you still want to go riding or . . ."

"I want to go riding," said Tessy quickly changing her expression to a sad face. The next day at school Olivia and Violet took Emma to the library. When they arrived the only other people there were three boys and the librarian. "Ms. Petunia come here!" Shouted Violet. The librarian rushed over to greet them. "Hi Violet, Hi, Olivia, what can I help you with?"

"Nothing! We would like you to meet our friend Emma." Ms. Petunia shook Emma's hand. "It is very nice to meet one more young, creative girl." The door opened and a tall girl with short hair walked in. "I must go help Abby," Ms. Petunia said. "Hey! Andrew, Benny, Devin, over here," said Mckenna. The three boys they had seen earlier walked over to the girls. "What's Up?" Asked Devin.

"Nothing. We just wanted to say hi and introduce you to our new friend, Emma."

"Nice to meet you," exclaimed Benny cheerfully. "You too!" Said Emma. As the girls left the library Emma tripped over what looked like an old, dusty book. "Are you okay?" Asked Violet. "I am, but what about the book?"

"What book is it?" asked Olivia. "I really can't even tell because of all the dust on it." Emma blew all of the dust off and all she could see was the Statue of Liberty. "WOW!" Exclaimed Emma. "Can we bring this book back to class to study The Statue of Liberty?"

"We have to check it out," said Violet. "Ms. Petunia!" Called Olivia. "Can we check out this book?"

"Sure, which book is . . . I've been looking for this book a long time and I had never found it. You guys are amazing!" Said Ms. Petunia. "Would you girls please come help me in the library every Friday afternoon?"

"Sure," said Mckenna. "Okay then. I will see you Friday," said Ms. Petunia. "Bye!" Said Violet as they walked out of the library. When Emma got off the bus, Tessy and her friend Maddie, were just getting off their bus. "Tessy!" Emma called. Tessy looked around and begin running towards Emma. "Come!" Tessy yelled to Maddie. While Tessy was right next to Emma, Maddie was running over. She tripped and fell and started to cry. Emma rushed over to Maddie and scooped her up. "Let's take her to our house," said Emma. When they arrived at the house, Emma took Maddie to her room where Sandy was playing with a pillow. Emma put Maddie down on the bed and got her a band aid.

"Mom!" Emma called. "Maddie is in my room and I have to bring Sandy out for a walk. Will you take care of Maddie?"

"Sure," answered Mom. Emma took Tessy and Sandy and placed Tessy in her stroller and put Sandy's leash around the handle of the stroller. "Here we go!" Exclaimed Emma. She started to push the stroller and right when she got out of the driveway Tessy saw Olivia and a small labradoodle. "Olivia!" Tessy yelled. "Tessy, Olivia is not here," said Emma. "Emma!" Olivia called. Olivia and the dog ran over. "Hey," said Olivia. "Who's the dog?" Asked Emma. "This is Cassie. She is mine,"

Said Olivia. Just then Sandy started to bark and Cassie stood, barking a little bit but standing still next to Mckenna. "Sandy!" Emma called. She picked Sandy up and unclipped her leash. Well I better get home to help my dad. "Bye!" Said Olivia. As Emma kept walking, she saw Maddie and Mom. Maddie was riding another horse we have, Lightning, and Mom was riding Thunder. "Mommy! Can Emma take me and Sandy home?" Asked Tessy. "Sure!" Mom answered.

When Emma got back to the house, Maddie's mom and sister pulled into the long driveway. Emma invited them into the house. "Hey!" Said Emma. "Hi!" Exclaimed Sarah, Maddie's sister. "Hi.," said Maddie's mom. Just then, they heard a sound coming from the barn. "You can wait here," Emma told Maddie's mom and Sarah. "I'll come," said Sarah. Emma picked up Tessy and the two girls ran to the barn. Maddie and Mom were just putting the horses away.

"Hi Sarah!" Screamed Maddie. She ran and gave her sister a big hug. "Hi! We gotta go," said Sarah. Dad just got back from vacation and he wants to see you."

"Okay. Let's go!" Said Sarah. She scooped Maddie up and ran to the car. "Hey mom," asked Emma. "Can I invite Violet and Olivia over to go for a ride?"

"Sure. But be sure to include Tessy and Dustin. Dustin won't want to go but i'm sure Tessy will."

Emma looked over at Tessy who was jumping up and down. "I'll call My friends." Emma took out her phone and dialed Violets number first. "Hi! It's Emma. I was wondering if you wanted to come over to ride horses with me." And she did the same thing for Olivia and they both said yes. Emma waited patiently for her friends to arrive. But as she waited she got tired. She decided to go get the horses ready. As she took a step into the barn, Olivia and Violet arrived. The girls knew that Emma said "riding" so they went straight to the barn. Right there at the entrance of the barn, Emma stood smiling. "Hi girls. Ready to ride? I've

228 • Nature & Nurture

got all the horses tacked up already so we can go riding right away. I was thinking ice cream," said Emma. "Yay!" Said Violet. They got on the horses and Violet was so excited this is what she said . . ." C'mon Boomerang!" So Boomerang sped up and started to gallop.

Violet leaned forward and then caught her balance. Olivia, Emma and Tessy sped up to and went so fast that they caught up with Violet and Boomerang. Emma made a wall with Belle, and Olivia, Steel, Tessy and Captain made another wall so Violet and Boomerang could not go so past them. "Slow down!" Said Emma. "Sorry," Violet said back. When they turned around, they were at the ice cream shop. They tied their horses to the bike rack and went up to the ice cream counter. Violet ordered cookie dough with whipped cream, and caramel, Emma ordered mint chocolate chip with chocolate sprinkles, and Olivia ordered chocolate soft serve with Rainbow sprinkles.

"Mmmm!" Violet said as she took a giant lick of her ice cream. Somehow Belle appeared behind the girls and sniffed Emma's hair. "How did Belle get undone from the bike rack?" Questioned Emma. "What about the other horses?" The girls stared at each other for a second and then took off running. Luckily, the horses were still there. "I think we better go home." When they got back home. They put the horses away and went inside. "Bye," Emma said as her friends pushed the heavy door open and stepped onto the pavement. "Yes!" Violet and Olivia said after school the next day. They were on The Kennedy Breakers. Aka: The school soccer team. The score was 13 to 4. "Our team was gonna win the tournament. Yahoo!" Emma yelled, standing on the thick, white sidelines. That must have gave the other team courage because they scored the second Emma stopped cheering.

The other team was one of the best teams in our town. They were called the Wilson crushers. They had never lost a game in their whole time playing soccer. Just then, everybody took a knee. Someone had gotten hurt. "Substitution!" The ref yelled. But nobody had a substitution. Olivia waved and then motioned for Emma to come substitute. Emma looked worried but she went into the field and Violet and Olivia's coach came out on the field, gave Emma a jersey and pointed to the porta-potty. A couple minutes later Emma ran back onto the field wearing a jersey with the number 13 printed boldly on the back of the shirt. She got into her place and the game started once again. Violet stole the ball and kicked it right to Emma. Emma juked number 3 on the Crushers and ran to the goal. She kicked the ball with all the power she had left in her and it went through the goalie's legs and went straight into the goal!

BUZZZZZZ!

"We won!" The breakers yelled as they ran to the middle of the field. They stood where the big tiger head laid on the grass. Emma gave her friends a big hug. The coach of the team walked quickly over to Emma. "Hi! I forgot to introduce myself," I am Coach Skyler. "Hi, I am Emma. I am Olivia and Violet's friend," Emma explained. "I don't want to make this an immediate decision, but since you won us the championship against a team that never lost this season, would you like to join the Breakers?" Asked Coach Skyler. "Sure!" Exclaimed Emma. "I love soccer anyway."

After School, the girls went to Violet's house. "I can't believe we won that game," Emma said. "Unbelievable," Violet said. Just then Tessy and Violet's sister, Mckenna, came into Violet's bedroom. "What are you doing here?" Emma asked Tessy. "I met Mckenna at school. We are best friends now," answered Tessy. "Congratulations!" Said Emma. "Your first best friend in town." Tessy went to sit on Emma's lap and Mckenna sat on Violet's. "I wish I had a sister," said Olivia.

"Olivia!" Violet's mom called. "Your mom is here." Olivia's brother Zach entered the room a minute later. "Time to go!" Zack said patiently. "But a brother is great too," said Olivia as she left the room. The girls went to the window just in time to see the black van pull carefully out of the driveway. "Well," Emma started to say, "we should play with the littles."

"Now that Olivia is gone," Violet added. The older girls played house and dolls with the younger girls until Emma and Tessy's mom arrived at the front door. "Bye!" Violet exclaimed as Tessy and Emma walked through the arch of the door. When the girls got to their car, there mom asked a simple question: "How was school today?" Emma answered right away. "Awesome! I joined the soccer team and won against a team that never lost."

"Wow Emmy. Impressive!" Mom answered. "Tessy? How was your day?"

"I made a new best friend. It is Violet's sister. Her name is Mckenna."

"Cool! It sounds like you both had a great day."

"Yeah!" Emma and Tessy said together. When they got home, their housekeeper, Ms. McElaney. "I just finished cleaning," she said. "Thank you so much." My mom gave her a 40 dollar bill and she left. Emma went up to her room and sat down on her bed to pet Sandy. Just then, Tessy and Dustin ran past Emma's door. Emma looked weird for a second and then wondered if this was a dream. She slowly started to tread out of the room. She peeked out of her room and guess what she saw? Tessy and Dustin playing barbie and car together. Emma went over to her siblings and asked this:

"What are you guys doing? Is this a trap?" Emma asked nervously and quickly. "We are playing and no," Tessy answered. From downstairs the kids could hear Sandy barking loudly. "BRB," Emma said. She raced down the steps almost tripping but caught her balance. Emma's mom was stumbling to get into the house but with Sandy in her way, she could not get in. Emma scooped Sandy up and began scratching her back. Sandy lowered her bark soon into a silent sound. "Good girl," Emma said placing Sandy back down on the wooden floor.

"Up! Up! And away!" Dustin said running past with Tessy right on his tail. "What are they doing?" Mom asked. "I asked the same question," Emma said, rushing back upstairs.

[Ding Dong]

"I will get it!" Said Mom. "Hi!" Emma heard her mom say. "Thank you! Bye." Emma listened closely to the sound of the door shut. Emma's mom came straight up to Emma's room. "Hi! You forgot this at school." Mom explained. She threw Emma the jersey. "Thanks," Emma said catching the shirt. Her mom shut the door and walked down the stairs.

The following day, Emma arrived at school early to practice soccer with Violet and Olivia. She spied not only her friends, but she also saw Devin too. The boy who she had met in the library. Then she spotted Andrew and Benny playing pass at the goal. Benny shot and it went into the goal. "Goal!" Emma yelled to get everybody's attention. "Emma!" Violet screamed on the top of her lungs so Emma could hear her. Violet passed Emma the ball. She kicked and hit the crossbar. Olivia was wearing her jersey. She waved to Emma and then turned around and kicked her ball to Devin. Olivia was number 24. She was one of the best players on the team. Just then a strong looking boy came over. With 2 other boys behind him he yelled, "What dorks! They can't even score a goal!"

Olivia, Violet and the boys gathered together. But Emma was not scared at all. She quickly placed the ball down on the turf and backed up. "Bruce," One of the boys behind the tough guy said. He did not pay attention though because he was too busy trying to be cool. Emma backed up more and aimed at Bruce. She ran forward and punted the ball straight at him. The ball soared through the air at a perfect speed. When the ball reached Bruce, it dropped down and hit him in the back. "Owwww!" He said. "That is payback for being rude to my friends." Bruce and the two boys ran away as fast as they could. Emma ran and high-fived all of her friends. "That will hopefully teach him a lesson,"

Emma said. "Now to get back to real soccer," said Emma glaring at Bruce who crossed his arms.

"Hey, do you guys all want to come over to my house to study?" Emma asked. "Sure!" Everyone answered. Mckenna was the last one at Emma's home. Minutes later, a girl showed up at the door with a dog on a leash. Emma ran downstairs to open the door. The second Emma opened the door. Olivia said, "I thought the dogs would want to play together."

"Sure," said Emma, winking at her new friend. Olivia unleashed Cassie. The girls and the dog walked up the stairs together. When they arrived in Emma's room everybody was there and even Sandy had come out of her hiding spot. Sandy had settled in on Violets lap with her head resting on her legs. Emma and Olivia walked over and sat down next to Violet and Tessy. The girls settled into the conversation pretty quickly because they were talking about soccer. "I play Kinder Kicks soccer!" Said Tessy excitedly. "Me too!" Said Dustin loudly. "I got a great idea!" Emma said. "We can go out in the backyard and play soccer. Girls versus boys!"

"Awesome idea!" Said Benny. "You girls are gonna get crushed!"

"I think not!" Answered Olivia smiling at Benny. As the kids went outside, Emma got behind grabbing a blue soccer ball out of a bin. She rushed to her position and the game started. Olivia kicked the ball through Andrews legs and passed the ball to Tessy who was standing near the goal. Tessy turned around and kicked the ball as hard as she could and it went into the goal slightly missing it. Violet ran to Tessy and ducked down. Tessy hopped onto Violets back. She ran down the field with Tessy singing. "You jinxed it! We are winning!" Tessy yelled when she passed Devin. Devin laughed as Tessy said that. Violet stopped and Tessy jumped of. Suddenly, Emma's mom came into the backyard with the tiniest horse the kids have ever seen.

"Great news! Lightning just had a foal!"

Emma and Tessy ran over. The spotted brown and white foal had big brown eyes and small hooves that would barely stand on the ground. He had a short mane laid flat on his neck. "We are thinking of calling him Champion." Explained Emma's mom. "We also got a letter from Olivia's parents." Emma took the letter and read out loud. "Hi Emma. This is Mrs. Carter. I would like to tell you that Olivia and Violet have been very good friends and since you just moved here, we are trying to make you feel at home. Please come over to our house whenever you feel like you need some company. We hope you will get to know Olivia and all of her friends and siblings better.

Love, Olivia's Parents"

"I feel so much more at home," said Emma brushing her hair out of her face. "Wow!" Said Olivia. "I did not expect that from my parents."

Well, I think we should take a ride into town. We can walk around, shop," Violet said completely changing the subject. "Sure," said Andrew. "I will go too," said one person slowly after another. "We can take the horses," Emma said. "I do not know how to ride," said Benny. "You will get used to it once you get to know me," Emma replied.

When the kids had mounted the horses, Emma led them to a little entrance through the bushes. She led her friends down the street and up the road until the got to what looked like a obstacle course. "I have a little shortcut," Emma said. She kicked Belle and the big brown horse sped up. The others copied. The kids jumped and turned there horses around until they reached the small town. The trotted up and down the street shopping and having fun. Just then, Devin spotted a man wearing a long black raincoat and sunglasses that was staring right back at them. Suddenly, he slowly moved closer and closer to where the kids where standing. He finally reached them and shook each one of their hands. "Hi. I am Ryan Alden. I think I know your mom. Jessie, right?"

"Yes. And how exactly do you know my mom?"

"I work with her. I would love to buy the gorgeous horse you are riding," Ryan asked. "No way!" Emma said. "This is my horse."

"$1,000,000?" Ryan asked not paying attention to Emma. Emma shook her head and made Belle start to walk again. It was silent for a couple seconds. "That was strange," Violet said breaking the silence. "Why would someone want to buy your horse. And he was wearing weird clothes for a warm day like today."

"I don't understand that guy yet. But we are gonna find out what's up," Emma said looking back at Olivia and Violet. Olivia spotted an apple tree near the park. "Let's tie our horses up there," she said. The girls looked at horse equipment at the store. When they returned to the apple tree. The spied Belle untied from the tree and Ryan Alden holding Belle's leash. They saw Benny standing across from him. He took out his phone and showed it to Ryan. Benny started to dial a number. Finally, Ryan handed Belle's leash over to Benny. Emma, Violet and Olivia ran back to the tree.

"What happened?" Emma asked giving Belle a hug. "Well," Benny started. "We were playing with a football when Mr. Ryan Alden snuck over and untied Belle from the tree. I spotted Belle with the corner of my eye. I ran over and started to dial the police department's number. Then he handed Belle over to me." Emma gave Benny a hug. "Thank you!" Emma said. "If I had lost Belle I would have died!" Belle nuzzled Emma in the shoulder. "I think he wants to go home," Emma said.

Olivia loaded up the bag connected to Belle's saddle. They started to move home. This time talking about how suspicious Ryan Alden was. When all the kids had left Emma's house, Tessy came out wearing pink from her headband to her shoelaces. She spied Emma in the barn and ran over. Emma had just finished putting the horses away. "Let me guess," Emma said turning around to look at Tessy. "You want a piggyback ride around the meadow?" Tessy nodded. When Emma finished Tessy's piggy-back ride she raced Tessy to the house. Emma sat down at the kitchen table.

Her mom was making tacos. "Mom?" Asked Emma. "Yes, sweetie?" Answered mom. "We met this mysterious man at town. He said he knew you. Ryan Alden?" Said Emma. "He was trying to make us sell Belle to him."

"I actually have no clue what you are talking about," Mom said. "He knew your name," Emma said rolling her eyes. "Ok," said Emma's mom. "He used to help me work with all of our horses, including Belle."

"So he knew Belle?" Emma asked curiously. "Yes. He did. Belle was his favorite horse. He used to spend hours a day play-ing with Belle. He loved Belle. But Belle did not love him back," explained Emma's mom. "But at that time, Belle had just been born. He was only a foal."

"Then Belle is his horse. I should have sold Belle to Ryan," Emma said sadly gazing down at the floor. "No sweetie. Belle is your horse. You are gonna keep him as long as he lives," Mom said brushing Emma's hair out of her eyes. "Really?" Emma said perking up a little bit. "Really," Mom said smiling at her daugh-ter. Emma got up and ran out the door. She ran so fast she blew the wind the opposite way. She quickly opened Belle's stall door again. She hopped onto him and led him to Olivia's house. She clung onto Belle's mane as she took off like a rocket. She ran past cars and houses of all sizes. When she finally reached the big blue house, she jumped off Belle and rang the doorbell. She waited a few seconds and then the door knob turned. Waiting at the door, was a young woman. She looked about sixteen years old. "Hi," She said. "I am Allie Winters. I am Olivia's babysitter."

"Hi," Emma said. "I am here to see Olivia. She needs to come with me somewhere." "No problem!" Said Allie. "Olivia!" She called. Emma heard fast footsteps coming down the stairs.

Emma was eager to talk to Olivia about Belle's story. Finally, Olivia peeked out the door. Emma waved. "Hi Emma!" Olivia exclaimed. "Can you come with me? Please?" Emma asked. Olivia ran back into the house. She returned seconds later with her jacket and shoes. She stepped out the door and onto the paved steps. Emma let Olivia sit behind her on Belle. They chatted about what had had happened to Belle when he was at the start of a new life. Emma told her all about how Ryan used to know Belle. Olivia was very surprised to hear that. An hour later, Emma dropped Olivia of back at her house. "Thanks for telling me that." Olivia said as she shut the door behind her. When Emma got home, she settled Belle in his stable and ran back to her house. She ran upstairs and sat on her bed. There was something weird about Ryan Alden and Emma and her friends were gonna find out.

To be continued . . .

Made in United States
North Haven, CT
04 September 2024

56742148R00143